The Pearl of Great Price

POPE PIUS VI (1717–1799)

THE PEARL OF GREAT PRICE

Pius VI & the Sack of Rome

BY CHRISTIAN BROWNE

Iterum simile est regnum cælorum homini negotiatori, quærenti bonas margaritas. Inventa autem una pretiosa margarita, abiit, et vendidit omnia quæ habuit, et emit eam.

Mt. 13: 45-46

AROUCA PRESS

2019 © by Arouca Press
© Christian Browne

All rights reserved:
No part of this book may be reproduced or transmitted,
in any form or by any means, without permission

ISBN: 978-1-9991827-9-3 (pbk)
ISBN: 978-1-7770523-3-1 (hardcover)

Arouca Press
PO Box 55003
Bridgeport PO
Waterloo, ON N2J3G0
Canada
www.aroucapress.com
Send inquiries to info@aroucapress.com

Book and cover design
by Michael Schrauzer
Cover image:
Pope Pius VI Taken Prisoner in 1798

*Hic liber consecratur
ad honorem Sanctissimae Trinitae
et scribitur cum gratiarum actione
propter donum fidei, sine quo nihil
habemus; et in devotione ad familiam
meam, uxorem et liberos.*
A M D G

TABLE OF CONTENTS

AUTHOR'S NOTE..................................XI
PROLOGUE XIII

ACT I: THE DEATH OF DUPHOT.................. 1
SCENE I
  The Palazzo Corsini, Rome, Christmas Night, 1797 3
SCENE II
  The Palazzo Corsini, 27 December 1797 (Morning) 9
SCENE III
  The Via Lungara, Outside the Palazzo Corsini,
  27 December 1797 (Evening) 11
SCENE IV
  The Quirinal Palace, Residence of the Pope,
  27 December 1797 (Night) 19

ACT II: THE FALL OF ROME....................25
SCENE I
  With the French Ambassador's Party at Florence,
  30 December 1797................................. 27
SCENE II
  Paris, Ambassador Bonaparte, with Desiree Clary,
  at the Home of Talleyrand.......................... 29
SCENE III
  The Luxembourg Palace, Meeting Place of the Directory,
  11 January 1798................................... 33
SCENE IV
  The Papal Residence at the Quirinal, 14 January 1798 39
SCENE V
  The Residence of Cardinal Somaglia, 15 January 1798....... 43

SCENE VI
> The Headquarters of General Berthier at Civita Castellana,
> 8 February 1798 49

SCENE VII
> The Vatican, the Evening of 8 February 1798 55

SCENE VIII
> At the Vatican, the Morning of 9 February 1798 57

SCENE IX
> At the Vatican, 10 February 1798 61

SCENE X
> General Berthier's Camp at Mount Mario, Outside Rome,
> 11 February 1798 65

SCENE XI
> At the Vatican, Just Before Midnight, 11 February 1798 69

SCENE XII
> Doria and the Pope, Midnight, 12 February 1798 71

SCENE XIII
> The French at the Roman Forum and the Pope at St. Peter's,
> 15 February 1798 73

SCENE XIV
> At the Vatican, the Evening of 15 February 1798 79

SCENE XV
> Azara's Apartments, 16 February 1798 85

SCENE XVI
> At the Vatican, 17 February 1798 91

SCENE XVII
> In the Sistine Chapel, the Morning of 19 February 1798 95

SCENE XVIII
> At the Vatican, Before Dawn, 20 February 1798 103

ACT III: THE POPE IN EXILE.................107

SCENE I
    At the Certosa, the Carthusian Monastery,
    Florence, 15 February, 1799.......................109

SCENE II
    Inside the Hotel du Gouvernement at Valence, France,
    28 August, 1799................................115

SCENE III
    At Valence, Spina and Napoleon, 11 October, 1799........119

EPILOGUE...................................125
BIBLIOGRAPHY..............................127
ABOUT THE AUTHOR.......................129

AUTHOR'S NOTE

When taking account of one's life, one is apt to feel like Caesar, weeping as he compared his accomplishments against those of Alexander the Great. This little book, I hope, will be an accomplishment in so far as it brings from obscurity the events it recounts and contributes to the understanding of the situation in which the Roman Catholic Church finds itself more than two centuries after the close of the story told in these pages.

This is the story of the last two years in the life of Pope Pius VI and the momentous occurrences that afflicted the Church in the final phase of the French Revolution, just prior to Napoleon's accession to power. The events recounted here are true. While the dialogue of the "characters" is the work of fiction, the scenes are drawn largely from historical accounts and, in most instances, reflect the spirit of what these individuals actually said and did. Certain lines are actual quotations from letters or memoirs, and I have made use of actual decrees and documents published at the time that these events unfolded. Since the book is, in part, a history, there are footnotes throughout to explain to the reader the sources from which the scenes are created.

In the incoherent era in which we live, where the influence of the Church has never been less formidable, the pope is, nonetheless, regarded as a kind of oracle whose only obstacle to sainthood is the beating of his heart. Thus, it is strange that the heroics of Pius VI (and those of his successor Pius VII) are so little known today. Both of these men, the "Prisoner Popes" of the French Revolution and Napoleonic Empire, stood in defiance of the hostile force of governments who wished either to control or destroy the Church. Both men endured physical torments, arrest, isolation and imprisonment for the sake of Religion.

Yet, unlike, for example, St. Thomas More, the modern Church does not extol the Prisoner Popes. More is now re-cast as the hero of conscience, fitting nicely into the Liberal conception that a man should not be compelled to participate in activity he subjectively finds repugnant. The American Bishops invoke More as the model of modern "religious liberty."

Pius VI, who died in exile, a prisoner of Revolutionary France, is, on the contrary, hardly known. Pius' story is not so easily co-opted by the Church of the era of the Second Vatican Council, for he stood against "democracy" as presented by the Revolution and its creed of Liberty, Equality and Fraternity. His cause was, in part, devoted to the maintenance of the temporal rights of the popes, a proposition of embarrassment to the post-Vatican II enlightenment.

His papacy also marks the beginning of the erection of the "Fortress Church," the Church closed-off against modernity that, in the mid-twentieth century, was the locus of such consternation to the "reformers." It was the windows of this Fortress, built in the wake of the calamities that befell Pius VI, that so many churchmen enthusiastically threw open, wholly forgetting why they had been shut in the first place.

This story, therefore, is a sort of beginning for the self-understanding of the Church in the 21st century. The common depiction of the Fortress Church is that of an institution of irrational reactionaries who foolishly protested against enlightened modernity. The culminating events of the life of Pius VI, however, help to explain the historical realities that caused the Church to attempt to close itself against the ideologies that dominate the thought of Modern Man. Those who bemoan the errors that befell the Church following the Second Vatican Council may gain new perspective by realizing that these follies plagued the Church long before 1962.

Finally, all who tend to lose heart in the face of a dismal state of ecclesial affairs can take solace from the way in which these imperfect men of the past weathered far greater threats than we know today with a singular focus on the primacy of Religion over all other interests and institutions and a devotion to the Traditions of the Church to which they deemed themselves servants. They knew the Pearl of Great Price.

PROLOGUE

On 4 May 1789, the meeting of the Estates General of France opened with a grand Eucharistic procession attended by the clergy, nobles and commoners, with the Archbishop of Paris holding the Sacrament aloft in a monstrance as the King and Queen of France followed behind him.

Little more than a month later, the majority of representatives of the First Estate — the clergy — joined themselves to the Third Estate, against the nobles and most of the bishops, in the singular event that precipitated the fall of the *ancien régime* and the commencement of the Revolution. It is one of the great ironies of history that the Church in France made the Revolution possible, and it was the Church in France that would become the institution most despised by the Revolution, a force that, in all its forms and phases, sought to control, subjugate and even eliminate the Christian Religion.

It fell to the aristocratic and worldly Pope Pius VI to confront the unprecedented assault upon the Church and Religion unleashed and sustained by the Revolution. From the outset, Pius VI was appalled by the events in France and early-on became an unequivocal and public opponent of the Revolutionary ideologies. In 1791, he thoroughly condemned the Revolutionary government's creation of the so-called "Constitutional Church", essentially a French national church with only a nominal connection to the See of Peter, and forbade the French clergy from swearing the required oath of allegiance to the Revolutionary government and this new, independent Gallican church.

Tragedies, horrors and disasters afflicted the Church in France relentlessly from 1790 onward, but no act threatened its beating heart as did the French invasion of northern Italy in the spring of 1796. The French armies, under the leadership of the young General Napoleon Bonaparte, drove the Austrians from Milan, and were positioned to move south towards a defenseless Rome, where the pope reigned not just as the Supreme Head of the Church, but as the prince of the Papal States, the dominions of central Italy that Peter's successors had ruled for 1,000 years.

At the time that Napoleon entered Milan, the Revolutionary government in Paris was under the control of the Directory, a body of five "consuls" who were the executive authority of the nation that, since its execution of the King and Queen in 1793, styled itself the French Republic. Dominated by anti-Christian Jacobin fanatics, the Directory was eager to spread the glories of liberty, equality and fraternity to all Europe. There could be no greater victory for the Revolutionary ideology than the conquest of Rome, whereby it would ensure the destruction of the pope's temporal power in favor of a new republic and perhaps even cause the end of the papacy itself.

Contrary to the desires of his masters at Paris, Napoleon did not proceed with haste to sack Rome. Instead, he invaded and took control over the "Legations", the northeastern part of the Papal States that included the cities of Ferrara, Bologna, Imola, and Cesena (the birth place of Pius VI and his eventual successor, Pius VII). Napoleon incorporated the Legations into a new nation he proclaimed as the Cisalpine Republic, with Milan as its capital.

On 17 February 1797, Pius VI signed the Treaty of Tolentino, by which he formally surrendered the Legations to Napoleon's new republic, and paid over heavy sums of treasure, both in money and works of art. The pope had almost no ability to resist, and could only hope his acquiescence would spare Rome itself.

Yet, in a foreshadowing of the defiance he would show in the face of grave danger over the next three years, Pius refused Napoleon's demand at Tolentino that he grant France the exclusive right to exercise a veto against the election of future popes. This touched upon an essential matter of the Church's spiritual constitution, and on such a point Pius would not yield, regardless of the consequences.[*]

---

[*] The demand and refusal are described by E. E. Y. Hales in *Revolution and Papacy* (Eyre & Spottiswoode, London, 1960).

Napoleon relented, and, against the demands of the Directors in Paris, he did not invade Rome, leaving intact the pope's rule over the remaining lands of the Papal States in Italy. Napoleon was now, however, the father of a new nation, and took a keen interest in arranging its affairs. He modelled the Cisalpine constitution on the one then in effect in France, establishing a ruling Directory, abolishing titles and privileges of nobility and adopting the Revolutionary new-age calendar.

These measures resulted in implacable opposition from the great cardinal-archbishops of the Legations (Mattei and Gioannetti) who held the Sees of Ferrara and Bologna. They detested the republican government, its irreligious foundations and its implicit endorsement of the Revolution.

But the cardinal-bishop of Imola, Gregory Barnabas Chiaramonte, adopted a different tack. The mild-mannered Benedictine monk sought to accommodate the new government for practical reasons, in order to avoid the chaos and violence that would result from pitting the people of his diocese against a French army committed to the export of the Revolution. Cardinal Chiaramonte's charge was to preserve Religion even under the secular republic, to marry it to the New Age, the success of which, he believed, depended upon its foundation in Christianity. To his official stationary he appended the motto "Liberty, Equality and Peace in Our Lord Jesus Christ."*

In late 1797, the government of the Cisalpine elected to formally adopt the charter of the Revolution, the *Declaration of the Rights of Man*, as its *Credo*, thereby disestablishing Catholicism as the official religion and proclaiming neutrality towards religious practice. The legal endorsement of error—false and incorrect religious doctrine—was wholly contrary to the Church's fundamental conception of a properly ordered society; it could never be accepted by Her bishops, the principal teachers of the Faith.

Nonetheless, the republican forces demanded that the bishops of the former Legations issue pastoral letters in support of the

---

* As noted by Hales; *Revolution and Papacy*, p. 107

Declaration of the Rights of Man, under the theory that "the spirit of the gospel is founded on the maxims of Liberty, Equality and Fraternity, and is in no wise contrary to Democracy."*

In the face of the demands of the government, Cardinal Chiaramonte demurred. He did not publish a pastoral letter. He did, however, take the pulpit at the Mass of Christmas Day, 1797 to address the directive. Here, in a sermon that was remembered at Paris 20 years later in the rubble of Napoleon's defeat, Chiaramonte reversed the government's theme.† It is not the Gospel that is founded upon the republican maxims, but the republican maxims that are founded upon the Gospel. Only Christian virtue can profit democracy, because, unlike the people dominated by hierarchical government, the free choice accorded to the people of a democracy requires in a particular fashion their infusion with supernatural Grace and the sure guidance of Doctrine, lest they use their freedom unwisely or immorally. The ancient republics of Greece and Rome so admired by the reformers failed, for they pre-dated Christ and, therefore, lacked the Grace and Doctrine necessary for true flourishing.

"Ordinary virtue might, perhaps, suffice to guarantee the lasting prosperity of other forms of government. Our form requires something more. Strive to attain the full height of virtue and you will be true democrats. Fulfil the precepts of the gospel and you will be the joy of the Republic. Be good Catholics, and you will be good democrats."‡

Thus, the cardinal-bishop of Imola strove to baptize the Revolution and make peace on Christmas Day. Two days after he preached these words, events at Rome set in motion the fate of the papacy, Religion and the cardinal's own destiny.

---

* Hales (p. 108), quoting the order of the Cisalpine government.
† Abbé Gregoire, the most famous of the so-called "Constitutional Bishops", who believed to the end that Christianity and the Revolution were allies, translated the sermon into French and read it to its author in Paris, by then known as Pope Pius VII, after the pope was at long last liberated following Napoleon's fall.
‡ A quote from the sermon, as recorded by Hales (pp. 108–109).

Act I
THE DEATH OF DUPHOT

The Assassination of the French General Leonard Duphot, killed in a tumult by the pontifical soldiers, December 28, 1797, engraving by F. Philippoleau, 1875

SCENE I
The Palazzo Corsini, Rome
CHRISTMAS NIGHT, 1797

[*Following the establishment of the Cisalpine Republic, Napoleon's brother, Joseph, entered Rome as the French ambassador, taking up residence in the Palazzo Corsini palace in Rome's Trastevere section, not far from St. Peter's Basilica. Here, Joseph Bonaparte gathered French military men and other exponents of the Revolution, with orders from the ruling Directory government in Paris to foment upheaval in Rome.*]

[*General Leonard Duphot, a hero of Napoleon's campaigns in Italy, and his fiancée, Desiree Clary, the sister of Joseph Bonaparte's wife, to whom Napoleon himself was engaged before his relationship with Josephine, have joined the ambassador in residence at the Palazzo.*]

Desiree Clary: It is Christmas in Rome.

General Duphot: But not in Paris. In Paris it is simply the fifth day of Nivose, and before long it will be so here as well. One day, even in Rome, they will number the days as we do in Paris, just as they now do in the Cisapline Republic, when we banish the ancient superstitions of this dying age.

Desiree: Can they be so easily banished, Leonard? From this very place, it is only a half-hour's walk to the place of St. Peter's death. Religion has lived here for nearly 1,800 years.

Duphot: But the Romans groan for liberty! Just as France rose against the despotic King and the irrational Church, so the Romans will rejoice on the day that the doddering old man who rules them as "His Holiness" gives way to a republic of freedom, equality and reason. General Bonaparte has already freed the Legations from this despotism, and returned the ancient glory of Republican Rome to Romagna. This is the land, after all, of Brutus and Cato and Cicero.

Desiree: And it is the land of Caesar and Constantine and Francis of Assisi. It was the priests who resisted the Revolution at home; the priests and the bishops who would not swear allegiance to the state at the expense of Religion. And it is the doddering old Pius who would brook no compromise on the oath. Our Revolution could not crush the Church in France. We should expect no easier victory in Italy.

Duphot: The forces of progress may be slowed, but they cannot be stopped, and certainly not by a feeble old man without an army. The Romans will rally to us, you shall see. In fact, I shall prove it to you.

In just a few days now, before we wed, I suspect we shall see a rising of the Roman people. It will be the Roman people who will demand a new republic for themselves. They shall demand a future of reason and liberty, without the burdens, myths and darkness of the past! We Frenchmen who already know the glories of the new age shall only help this people claim for itself the rights that are its due.

In fact, we have arranged to have a great celebration here two days hence. We will fill the square and the streets around this palace. We will place the Republican colors all about, and we will invite the people to rejoice with us for the great blessings of liberty and equality that flow from our Revolution — blessings that have already come to Italy in the Cisapline Republic; and blessings that may soon come to the Romans themselves.

Desiree: You would see the Romans rise now, during Christmastide? Perhaps on the Feast Day of the Holy Innocents? If you are not careful, Leonard, many here, I fear, will suffer the fate

Act I, Scene I 5

of the children at the hands of Herod. You speak as if the guillotine was never dropped in Paris.

Duphot: And you speak for that which was neither holy nor innocent. You shall see how the Romans wish to join the new age! Regardless, they may keep their religion, if they wish, but they yearn to be free of the pope's temporal power, this medieval vestige of heredity, privilege and arbitrary authority. The Romans ought to govern Rome, as they did even before the birth of Christ.

Desiree: And if the Romans govern Rome, will France govern the governors?

Duphot: We will guide the people, we will secure their liberty, just as we have at home and just as we have in the north, in the Cisalpine lands. We will guide them by reason. Yes, they may maintain the Catholic religion if they so wish, but they will have no more rule by ecclesiastics.

Desiree: By whom shall they be ruled?

Duphot: We will make provisions for republican government when the people are ready.

Desiree: And while they wait, they will be subject to a new government to which they must be loyal, yes?

Duphot: Of course! It will be their own government, secured for them by our force of arms. Like any people, the Romans, and all of Italy, must submit to legitimate civil authority.

Desiree: Only civil authority? What of the rights of the Church?

Duphot: The Church may keep its rights, and its rites! The Directory is not the Convention. It does not seek to banish religion. Robespierre is dead, and we killed him, after all!

Desiree: But the Church will be subject to the new government.

Duphot: The Church is concerned with religion; the government with the general welfare. Thus, the Church's sphere of authority is merely a part of the greater whole of the general welfare, for which the civil government is responsible. So, yes, the Church will be under the state. The citizen is first loyal to the state. He may have his religion in order to cultivate his virtue, all for the purpose of doing his part for the general good under the auspices of the civil government.

Desiree: But here the Church is both religion and state. The state is the religion and the religion is the state. It is meant to reflect the rule of Christ. There is no separation because the faith rules in all matters, civil and religious, with the same force and effect.

Duphot: Nonsense. It cannot be so in modernity. Such a system is merely the despotism of the Dark Ages. The pope has no temporal power and never rightly did. There is no liberty, no reason in a government by religion. The purpose of religion is to make a virtuous citizenry. For that is it useful — perhaps even necessary. But it must serve the state and be administered by the state.

In any event, the civil authority is nothing but a burden on the Church. We would free it to tend to its spiritual purposes, with no need to concern itself with laws and armies and foreign affairs.

Desiree: The Revolution, it seems, will therefore foster the Christian Religion. How ironic: we must destroy it to save it, I suppose.

Duphot: If you like, yes. We would return the Church to its primitive glory. It will be as it was in the days of the Apostles and the Fathers, before the accretions and corruptions of later times.

Desiree: It is quite a thing, this Revolution. It restores the Republic of Scipio and the Church of St. Paul in one stroke — and all by deposing the pope as ruler in Italy. Perhaps we are even too modest; I think it is the greatest change of power in Italy since Aeneas' ship arrived from Carthage.

Duphot: You may be right, my dear. Something new and great has come to be in our age, something not seen since ancient times. We cast off the past, but restore it too. In the end, there will be a new religion — of liberty, reason and humanity. "Theophilanthropy" they now call it in Paris — all under a republic. The point is to make the citizens virtuous servants of the state, educated by reason, not superstition. Remember this night, for we have witnessed the passing of what may be the last Christmas in Rome, under the last pope.

Desiree: "Heaven and earth may pass away, but my words will not pass away." Be careful, General. Happy Christmas.

SCENE II

The Palazzo Corsini

27 DECEMBER 1797 (MORNING)

J. Bonaparte: Are your men ready, General?

Duphot: Yes, Ambassador. The soldiers will fill the square of the palazzo by noon and we shall gather a crowd, all wearing the tricolor cockade. Our men have already begun to spread the news across the city that there shall be a great celebration of the Revolution here tonight. By sunset, we shall assemble a great crowd — we shall march on the walls of St. Peter's if you tell us to do so!

J. Bonaparte: Do as you say. When the crowd assembles, we shall let it take its own way. Let the pope try to keep order over the city if he can. Let them come to this outpost of liberty under the pope's nose — and then let the crowd rule. Make sure your men have money enough to pay the shopkeepers near the palace so that the crowd may have food and wine, enough to keep the people reveling well into the night.

Duphot: And when the crowd cries out for you to address the people, Ambassador, will you come down?

J. Bonaparte: Yes, but I will admonish the crowd to keep in order. We must not appear to foment riots or the violent overthrow of the papal government. We cannot risk alarming the Austrians or the Neopolitans. If the royalist governments believe we plan to spread the Revolution by chaos and violence through all Italy, we may have war again from both the south and the north. England and Spain, too, might intercede against us.

So I must always demand calm and order in public. But if the people tear down the pope, so be it. Or, should the pope have his men attack French soldiers, then, of course, we must defend our men and our rights. But I am the ambassador. We have a treaty with the Papal States and we shall honor it. Let the pope break the peace, or let him be broken by his own people."

SCENE III

The Via Lungara, Outside the Palazzo Corsini
27 DECEMBER 1797 (EVENING)*

[*On the evening of 27 December 1797, a great crowd assembled up and down the Via Lungara, the street along the Tiber River leading out from the residence of Ambassador Bonaparte at the Palazzo Corsini.*]

[*French soldiers, under the command of General Duphot, distribute the tricolor "cockade," the ribbon worn on the lapel of a jacket, to symbolize loyalty to Revolutionary France. Other Frenchmen give coins to the people to enable them to purchase wine, encouraging a riotous atmosphere.*]

[*As the crowd grows, instigated by the French, some begin to shout protest slogans, decrying the injustices of the papal rule.*]

First Man in the Crowd: People of Trastevere! People of Rome! How much longer will we toil and sweat for pennies, while the pope and his cardinals live in opulence on the fruit of our labor, taxing us for their pleasure!

Woman in the Crowd: One week's wage hardly purchases a loaf of bread!

Second Man: Why must we be subject to the rule of the pope when the French rule themselves? This city belongs to the citizens, not the pope. Let us strip the gold from his palace and the jewels from his chalice and we will feed the people!

---

* Based upon the accounts of these events set forth in *A Journal of the Most Remarkable Occurrences that Took Place in Rome, Upon the Subversion of the Ecclesiastical Government, in 1798*, by Richard Duppa and *Epistolario of Jose Nicolas de Azara* (1784–1804).

First Man: "Render unto to Caesar what is Caesar's and unto God what is God's." The pope thinks he is Caesar, but even Caesar refused the crown. We are the true Christians. Let us rid ourselves of the corruption of the pope.

Another Man: "It is easier for a camel to pass through the eye of a needle than for a rich man to enter the Kingdom of Heaven." If we take their money, we shall help them to heaven! [*Laughter.*]

Franciscan Friar (a religious in the service of the French): My children, listen well. We are no mob, bent on the overthrow of our government. No, we are governed by the words of the Savior Himself.

"No man can serve two masters," says the Lord. But the pope serves Mammon with his taxes, his police and his palaces.

"My kingdom is not of this world," says the Lord. But the pope has a kingdom in this world while he neglects the spiritual welfare of his flock.

"My house shall be a house of prayer, but you have made it a den of robbers," says the Lord. This government uses our Holy Religion to rob the people of its little money, to live in luxury while you cannot even pay for a little bread, or oil, or other provisions!

No, we are no mob. We act in the name of Christ and at His commands. We would restore our rights and the true religion, the Church purified. So let us show the pope who is sovereign here! March to the Ponte Sisto. Take the bridge, cross the Tiber and on to the Quirinal. Just as the Parisians breached the walls of the Tuilleries and made the king a prisoner, so we Romans must take the pope from his palace!

[*The crowd proceeds along the Via Lungara to the Ponte Sisto, a short walk from the ambassador's palace. At the Ponte Sisto, it attempts to cross the Tiber and march to the pope's residence on the Quirinal Hill, but here papal troops on horseback block the way and push the crowd back across the*

Act I, Scene III 13

> bridge and towards the Corsini. As the crowd fills the street and the square in front of the Ambassador's palace, J. Bonaparte, along with Duphot and his men, come forth to address the people, while the papal police on horseback attempt to disperse the mob.]

Duphot [*sword in hand*]: Citizens! Citizens! Stay calm and listen. The Ambassador wishes to address you.

Papal Solider [*holding a musket*]: By order of the Cardinal Secretary of State, leave this place and return to your homes. The city will come to order. Leave this place. [*he fires into the air*]

Man in the Crowd: Where is Bonaparte? We will not leave until we see him! We are here to ask him to take control of Rome and rule the citizens. FREEDOM!

Lead Papal Solider: You will leave now! You have no right to assemble here.

The Crowd: FREEDOM! FREEDOM! FREEDOM!

Duphot [*waiving his sword*]: Citizens! Listen. The Ambassador will address you, but we must have calm. Please — make way, clear the square!

Papal Solider [*shouting over the crowd to Duphot*]: Drop your sword!

Duphot [*still waiving his sword*]: I am in command here. This square is under the jurisdiction of the French government. My men will restore order.

Another Papal Solider: Sir, the general is inciting the people! He brandishes a sword.

The Crowd: FREEDOM! FREEDOM! FREEDOM!

Lead Papal Solider: Put down your sword, sir, and return to the palace.

[*Fights break out among the papal soldiers and the crowd. Some attempt to pull the papal soldiers from their horses. Shots ring out from within the crowd and, at the sound of gunfire, people flee from the square in a panic.*]

French Soldier [*to J. Bonaparte*]: Sir, General Duphot is shot! He is lying the middle of the square.

J. Bonaparte: Duphot? Is he dead? Quickly, bring him into the palace. Order all of our men inside immediately and bar the doors.

[*The French soldiers collect Duphot's body and carry it into the palace. The Ambassador and his men retreat inside. The crowd disperses as the papal troops clear the square.*]

Bonaparte's Aide: Duphot is dead, sir. Most unfortunate. He was a fine general and as dedicated a citizen as any in France.

J. Bonaparte: Yes, this is indeed a pity. Duphot was my friend and a loyal lieutenant to my brother. None served in Italy with greater distinction. And on the eve of his wedding! I shall have to tell Desiree myself.

Aide: Ambassador, Señor Azara is here. He wishes to speak with you immediately.

[*Jose Nicolas Azara, the Spanish ambassador to the Papal States, counsellor to the Pope and mediator with the French, enters Bonaparte's residence, accompanied by two papal guards.**]

---

* Based upon Azara's account of his meeting with Joseph Bonaparte in a letter published in Azarar's *Epistolario*.

Act I, Scene III   15

Azara: Ambassador! Are you well? The city is in chaos! I received reports of the commotion and violence and went immediately to the Vatican. It is locked tightly and under heavy guard. I did not wait to see the pope, but came here straightaway with the help of these men. Otherwise I would not have been able to pass through the streets. What has happened here?

J. Bonaparte: A great riot has happened here, unleashed by radicals and the recklessness of the soldiers of this failing government. I was nearly killed by their indiscriminate violence. General Duphot was not so fortunate. He was cut down by the pope's men in front of me, right here in the square, in the jurisdiction of the French Republic.

Azara: I offer my condolences on behalf of my government, your Excellency. I should also like to offer my sincerest regrets to Miss Clary, a great lady. May I suggest that I accompany you to see the pope immediately?

J. Bonaparte: No, Señor, that will not be necessary. I witnessed soldiers under the authority of the papal government shoot and kill a French general, on French territory. I have no wish to see the pope. It is my duty now to leave for Paris at dawn and make a full report of these events to the Directory. It will fall to our government to decide how we will deal with the States of the Church in light of this reckless aggression.

Azara: But, Ambassador, I have been to the Vatican just an hour ago. Neither the pope nor the Curia know anything of these events. Surely you know, the pope did not order any such violence. He will be aghast to learn of General Duphot's death. Should you not, at least, speak to the papal government before you make your report to Paris?

J. Bonaparte: These events call for a response beyond my authority. I have done what I could to keep order here. The people wished for me to overthrow the pope; I refused. But the pope's men nonetheless killed a French general and a hero of the Revolution. How the Directory will decide I do not know, but, yes, it is true, Señor, that General Duphot longed to bring about an end to papal despotism. He may indeed have succeeded in so doing tonight.

[*Desiree Clary enters.*]

J. Bonaparte: Desiree, my dear, you have heard the news, I am afraid?

Desiree: Yes, Joseph, I learned of Leonard's death upon my return to the palace. It is most unfortunate, of course.

J. Bonaparte: Indeed. Desiree, I am leaving at dawn for Paris to give a full account of these events to the Directory. You shall return with your sister and me.

Desiree: What will happen to the Romans, Joseph?

J. Bonaparte: That is a matter for the Directory to decide. But I have every confidence that we shall not let the death of your fiancé pass until we have punished those responsible for it.

Desiree: Or until we destroy the States of the Church entirely, as Leonard wished to do

J. Bonaparte: We destroy it? No, Desiree, it is the spirit of the age that will destroy the secular power of the pope. Look around you! Rome rises against the Church. The Romans try to crown me a new Caesar. In the former dominions of the Church, the citizens of the new Cisapline Republic push further and further into the territory still under papal control. The ideals of the Revolution animate all Italy. Only tonight, here in the square, before Duphot was killed, the Romans shouted out "Freedom!

Freedom!" The Church and the papacy are already at an end. If the Directory makes what is already so manifest, it does a service to all men.

Desiree: Leonard spoke just as you do now to me on Christmas night. He was as sure as you, Joseph, that Rome would fall to the Revolution. But it is Leonard that has fallen, amidst violence and the tearing down of the order of the ages. His death may yet unleash more fury, and to what end? Invasion? The carting off of art and treasure? A new "freedom" that knows no purpose other than to destroy the past?

Azara: Miss Clary, you are speaking from your grief. I am certain your government will honor its commitment to peace and the good order of Italy.

Desiree: I am sorry for Leonard's death, but not for the death of our marriage. Joseph, I will leave with you and my sister tonight. I have no wish to see what will become of this city. I shall prepare my things. Good night, Señor Azara.

Azara: Good night, Miss Clary. Please again accept my condolences, and those of my government, on the loss of Gen. Duphot.

[*Exit Desiree Clary.*]

There is truth in what she says, Ambassador. I beg you again: see the pope before you leave. Do not go in haste and anger. More than just the fate of a city hangs now on what your government may do. We risk not just the end of the sovereign power of a ruler, but the destruction of the oldest institution in Christian Europe. Can there be a Europe at all without the papacy at Rome?

J. Bonaparte: My dear Azara, I am but an ambassador. The Directory shall decide who shall be master of Italy and what shall become of all Europe. But we have seen kings fall and institutions end. Man moves from ignorance towards reason and knowledge. He demands freedom and equality, and the forces that resist these ideals are necessarily crushed, based as they are on fables or privilege.

Once, it was the pope who humbled the emperor. It was the Church that ruled the state. For three days, a pope kept an emperor on his knees, in the frigid cold, waiting to beg the pope's forgiveness. That world is long over, wiped away by Reformation and religious war; science and a new philosophy and the enlightenment of man.

Now it is the pope who must beg for mercy, not from an emperor, but from the government of a new Republic that has thrown off the shackles of the old order in favor of liberty, equality and fraternity. It is these ideals that humble the pope and demand that he be ousted, not the death of any one man, even a general.

Return to the Vatican, Señor. Tell the pope I have departed, and shall not return until I receive instructions from Paris. Good night.

Azara: As you wish, Your Excellency. I wish you a safe passage home. Good night.

SCENE IV

The Quirinal Palace, Residence of the Pope
27 DECEMBER 1797 (NIGHT)*

[*Reports from the Palazzo Corsini of Duphot's death reach the papal residence at Quirinal Palace. The Cardinal Secretary of State, Guiseppe Doria Pamphili, along with Azara, bring the news to Pope Pius VI.*]

Pius [*reading a report handed him by Doria*]: Duphot is dead? Are you certain?

Cardinal Giuseppe Doria Pamphili (*Secretary of State*): Yes, Your Holiness. Several of our commanders saw him fall and saw the French drag his body inside the ambassador's palace. He is dead.

Azara: Of this there is no doubt, Your Holiness. I have been to the Palazzo Corsini only an hour ago. I saw the general's body myself.

Pius: We pity him. He died, no doubt, unrepentant of his crimes against the Church and his erroneous, impious beliefs. We shall pray for him. But how did he come to this end?

Doria: It is said he was brandishing a sword and shouting out to the crowd. There was great disturbance and shots were fired; he fell. None of our men has admitted to shooting him. Indeed, it is as likely that he was killed by a shot from his own soldiers or from some Jacobin maniac as it is that he was killed by our troops.

---

* In general, based upon the account of Azara in his *Epistolario*.

Pius: Send for Bonaparte tomorrow morning. We shall speak with him and We shall confirm our commitment to keeping order in the city. We shall offer our personal regrets at the general's death to the French government.

Azara: Your Holiness, I am afraid that will not be possible. The ambassador told me himself that he will leave Rome at first light, with his whole household, and return to Paris in protest against Duphot's death.

Doria: Return to Paris! Without seeing His Holiness?

Azara: I begged him to reconsider, but he was unyielding. He will leave now and report to the Directory what has happened here tonight. What will follow his report he does not know.

Doria: But what is it that he will report? This government gave no orders to permit harm to any Frenchmen, let alone to a general officer and intimate of the ambassador's family. Surely, Bonaparte knows as much! Why, it was the radicals who support the French who instigated this tragedy, not the papal government.

Azara: Nonetheless, a French general lies dead on the doorstep of the French ambassador's residence. Is it not apparent where the blame for the event shall fall? For several weeks now, the French have incited their Jacobin supporters in the so-called Cisalpine Republic to attack your borders in the north. They have already taken the Fortress San Leo, and they have ravaged all through the countryside. The last reports say these rioters have pushed down as far as Ancona, all on the excuse that Your Holiness has failed to recognize with due solemnity the legitimacy of the Cisalpine government. Duphot's death, it seems to me, provides a ready excuse for the Jacobins to continue their campaign to the gates of Rome.

Act I, Scene IV

Pius: And yet We have already conceded to the creation of this new republic carved out of Our former lands and at so great a price. They have exacted their tribute and carried off the treasures of the ancients that belong by right to the Roman people. And still they continue their violence, pushing ever onward, never satisfied until they have destroyed the entire patrimony of the Church.

Azara: Precisely, Your Holiness. And if they have continued to make war on such a flimsy pretext as your supposed failure to recognize their government in a fittingly obsequious manner, consider how much more they might do when armed with the excuse of the murder of a heroic solider of the Revolution.

Doria: Then we must try to placate Bonaparte. We must apologize for Duphot's death. Azara, go after him, find him on the road back across the Alps, wherever he may be, and offer the apology of the papal government.

Azara: If you apologize, Your Eminence, you concede papal responsibility for his death. I am sorry, Cardinal, but such a mission is beyond my remit as Spanish ambassador here. I cannot pursue Bonaparte for you; whatever you do with the French now, you must do directly.

Doria: Then I shall find him myself and deliver the apology. Your Holiness, what choice have we? If the French unleash their troops and the Jacobin destroyers on Rome, we have no defenses. The city would be crushed. It would mean the end of the states of the Church, of the independence of the Church. The Church will be placed under the heel of the boot of the godless destroyers of eighteen centuries of Christian life. Your Holiness, we must apologize. I see no other way.

Pius: Yes, Doria, perhaps we must, but We weary of these endless accommodations with those who would destroy Religion.

From the start, We have wished for peace with this Revolution. Perhaps We remained silent too long in the face of the indignities put upon the King and the Church. We have seen the Eldest Daughter of the Church transform herself into a hideous monstrosity — first with the detestable oaths forced upon the clergy; then by the barbarous execution of her King and Queen; the wanton killing of so many priests and religious women; even the attempt to expel the Christian Faith itself from her borders and replace it with the worship of "reason" — and the god of reason is the god of the guillotine.

Now these impious men ravage Our lands, the patrimony of the Church, and wish to destroy, even as they proclaim that they have come to restore. We have given the French all that We are able to give. They have taken Our temporal rights in Avignon and in the Legations; they have demanded Our gold and they have carted off sculpture and painting. But they have extracted nothing from the treasury of our Holy Religion, nor shall they do so, so long as any pope reigns, and it is Our solemn duty to protect and preserve Rome as the capital of Christendom.

So, go, Doria, apologize for Duphot's death and do whatever you can to assuage Bonaparte. We shall seek peace and pray for peace. But the French add to their many errors if they think that We shall concede the "smallest part of the smallest letter" to their barbarism.

Azara: Your Holiness must be prepared to flee the city. If the French come here, they must find this palace empty. For the good of the Church, Your Holiness, you cannot suffer the fate of Louis and Marie Antoinette.

Pius: The good of the Church, Azara? The blood of the martyrs is the seed of Christians. If Providence deems that Our death in this manner is necessary to save the Church from the evil of the Jacobins, FIAT! Tell me, Azara, is it right to give to another that which you do not own, even should the other demand it of you?

Act I, Scene IV

Azara: No, Your Holiness, to do so would transgress the Seventh Commandment. It would be stealing.

Pius: Indeed. We shall give to the French, to the Jacobins, to the impious, all that We possess — even Our own life. But We shall not give away that which does not belong to Us. We are the trustee and temporary custodian of these lands, not their owner, just as We are the temporary guardian of the Deposit of the Faith. It does not belong to the pope to dispose of the Church's patrimony as he pleases, whether a temporal or spiritual component of the inheritance bequeathed by Christ to His Apostles and they to their successors.

The pope has ruled Rome and these states for more than a thousand years. While Rome fell to the barbarians, the pope remained. Our predecessor Leo the Great alone kept alive both the Christian Faith and the Roman ways here, as the whole of the West crumbled. Even so, the popes remained still subject to the power of the Emperor in the East and the endless wars of the Lombards and the invaders from the north, until Pepin and Charlemagne gave these lands to Our predecessors, securing the rights of the Church such that the Church should never again be less than the civil power, but should stand as its equal, even its superior — just as the supernatural Faith is superior to the concerns of this world.

We shall not again place the Church beneath an emperor, even one that calls itself a "republic" and pretends at an enlightenment that is, in reality, the eclipse of the light of Truth. The Church does not belong to any one nation. Its mission is to preach the Gospel even unto the ends of the earth. The pope rules here not for his own power, but as Vicar of Christ, just as Christ is the true King in Heaven and on the earth.

The Church must never be reduced to a mere creature of the state. These lands guarantee that the Church will stand at least co-equal with every civil authority in the world. The papal lands are the manifestation of the fact that Christ's rule is on earth. He is the true sovereign that precedes and supersedes all the others. The pope is merely his vicar, His visible minister.

It is false and pernicious, therefore, to suggest that the temporal authority of the Church is a burden to Her mission or stain on Her purity or has no claim on modern man. So let them come, if it is God's will. But Rome We shall not abandon. We are bishop of the Roman See and the lawful sovereign of these lands — they belong to the Church, and We shall not give away that which We do not own.

Act II
THE FALL OF ROME

*The Entrance of the French Army into Rome,
15 February 1798,* by Hippolyte Lecomte, 1834

SCENE I
With the French Ambassador's Party at Florence
30 DECEMBER 1797

[*Upon leaving from Rome, Ambassador Bonaparte and his companions journeyed north to Florence, where they stopped to rest on the way to Paris. There, Bonaparte composes a detailed account of the events that lead to Duphot's death and sends a messenger carrying the account to the French Foreign Minister, Talleyrand.*]

Aide: Have you finished your dispatch, Ambassador? The messenger is ready to leave for Paris.

J. Bonaparte: It is nearly complete; I am just now reading a letter delivered to me moments ago from Ambassador Azara in which he relates that the pope and Doria are frantic for me to return to Rome. Azara simply confirms the complicity and duplicity of the papal government. Let me finish the dispatch as follows:

> This government is not inconsistent with itself. Crafty and rash in perpetrating crime, cowardly and fawning when it has been committed, it is today upon its knees before the minister Azara, that he may go to Florence and induce me to return to Rome. So writes to me that generous friend of France, worthy of dwelling in a land where his virtues and his noble loyalty may be better appreciated[*].

> Take this now to Paris, directly to Citizen Talleyrand. I pray the government will endorse our departure from Rome and see

---

[*] Correspondence of J. Bonaparte from Florence to the French government, as quoted by John S.C. Abbot, *The Story of Joseph Bonaparte*, Harper & Brothers Publishers, 1902.

the death of Duphot as the crime that it is. Tell the minister we await his response and further instructions.

> [*Ambassador Bonaparte and his party stayed at Florence, awaiting a reply from Paris. Within days, Talleyrand replies to Bonaparte, and directs him to continue on to Paris immediately.*]

Aide: Ambassador, a dispatch from Minister Talleyrand has arrived.

J. Bonaparte: Excellent. Give it to me now. [*reads*] I am directed to return to Paris as soon as possible and to go immediately to see the minister. He wishes to speak with me before he briefs the Directory on the matter of the papal government.

Aide: Do you have the minister's support, Ambassador? If he were not pleased, would he not instruct us to return to Rome?

J. Bonaparte: Indeed. I shall read to you from his reply:

> *I have received, citizen, the heart-rending letter which you have written me upon the frightful events which transpired at Rome on the 28th of December. Notwithstanding the care which you have taken to conceal everything personal to yourself during that horrible day, you have not been able to conceal from me that you have manifested, in the highest degree, courage, coolness, and that intelligence which nothing can escape; and that you have sustained with magnanimity the honor of the French name. The Directory charges me to express to you, in the strongest and most impressive terms, its extreme satisfaction with your whole conduct. You will readily believe, I trust, that I am happy to be the organ of these sentiments.**

Let us prepare to leave for Paris without further delay.

---

* Ibid.

SCENE II

Paris, Ambassador Bonaparte, with Desiree Clary at the Home of Talleyrand

Talleyrand: Welcome home, Ambassador. And welcome Miss Clary. On behalf of all France, let me extend our condolences to you on the death of General Duphot, a great hero of this Republic.

Desiree: Thank you, Minister. I am happy to be back in Paris.

Talleyrand: Come, Ambassador, we must talk before you see the Directory later today. I wish to prepare you for what is likely to come.

J. Bonaparte: Thank you, Minister. I am eager to listen.

Talleyrand: All of the members of the Directory have been in a frenzy these last 10 days, since we received the news of Duphot's death. You will pardon me, Miss Clary, but there are those for whom his death is a cause of some rejoicing, in the sense that he is a martyr for his country whose death may bring about the end of an odious institution — the papal government at Rome.

Desiree: I am not offended, Minister, nor surprised. Besides, the general himself would rejoice to know that the government might use his death to spread its revolution. Duphot wanted to end the pope's power just as much as I suppose the Directors do. I hear that while we have been away in Rome, the Directory has busied itself furthering the latest new religion for the people. Is it not so?

Talleyrand: Yes, it is the great project of the new Directors. You were absent during the coup on 18 Fructidor — that is, 4th September of this past year, as I suppose you are used to the old calendar still in use at Rome. On that day, the Director La Revelliere, along with the Directors Barras and Rewbell, removed the two Directors whom they believed to have royalist sympathies. They were replaced by Philippe Merlin de Douai and Nicolas-Louis Francois de Neufchateau.

The point, my dear, is that these new men are absolutely committed to a new religion that is to be compulsory for the whole citizenry. They called it "Theophilanthropy." It worships the state and the civic virtues.

Desiree: You mean it is man worshipping himself.

Talleyrand: Touché! How true! As I say, Jesus Christ, to found his religion, was crucified and resurrected; Revelliere should try to do the same.[*] But you must know, however absurd it may seem, these five Directors excel even Robespierre in their desire to see the Christian Religion entirely supplanted. There is no greater symbol of the Christian Faith than the pope, and these men need little prompting to destroy him, especially with our forces already at his doorstep.

J. Bonaparte: Am I to report to them in a manner designed to try to save the pope? I have no wish to countermand the prejudices of the Directors. Besides, the stupidity of the papal government nearly cost me my life. I will not attempt to be its apologist.

Talleyrand: No, Ambassador, you will not. You will affirm your account of the attack on your embassy and the death of Duphot — and that is all you will do. Your task is to survive in the service of this government, until we shall have another,

---

[*] A quote Talleyrand attributes to himself in his memoirs, *La Confession de Talleyrand*, V. 1-5, *Memoires du Prince Talleyrand*.

Act II, Scene II

just as I have done: once a bishop of the Roman Church, now the minister of a government devoted to its destruction.

Desiree: Was it a long journey, Minister, from the miter to the tricolor?

Talleyrand: The path to survival is always the shortest one, Miss Clary. I regret to say that suffering disgusts me, misery disgusts me, all that is ugly and vulgar inspires me with insurmountable repulsion.* And so I learned to avoid these things and to prosper where others fled, were shot, sent to prison colonies or lost their heads.

Joseph's report may well end 1,000 years of papal rule as swiftly as the last coup d'etat ended two years of rule by the first Directors. Now we have new Directors, and, someday, their foolishness will end their rule — perhaps in a year, perhaps in 1,000 years. It matters not to me, so long as I do what must be done as it regards my own life. I am man of the practical, not a man of "ideology," a new term our Director Reveillere is proud to tell you he invented. But, enough of this talk for now. It is time, Ambassador, to leave for the Luxembourg Palace and make your report to our board of Caesars.

---

* Ibid., another quote from Talleyrand.

SCENE III

The Luxembourg Palace, Meeting Place of the Directory
11 JANUARY 1798

[*Talleyrand accompanies Ambassador Bonaparte to the Luxembourg Palace, the meeting place of the Directory. All five of the Directors assemble to hear the ambassador's report.*]

Director Barras: Welcome, Citizen Ambassador. We are pleased you have returned to France.

J. Bonaparte: Thank you, Citizen Director. It is an honor to have an audience before you. I am at your disposal to give an account of the events in Rome that led to the death of General Duphot and my return here.

Director La Revelliere: We have read your reports, Citizen, and we have already heard from the Citizen Foreign Minister on the general's death. We did not call you here to hear you repeat what we already know.

Director Barras: We wish to commend you on your service to the Republic. You shall not return to Rome, Ambassador. We would like you to go to Berlin as ambassador as soon as you are able.

J. Bonaparte [*looking at Talleyrand*]: Why, I am honored, Citizen Directors. I had hoped to stay in Paris and serve the government here. Perhaps I will consult on the matter with my brother. But what of Rome? What is to be done about the papal government?

Director La Revelliere: What, indeed, of the papal government? Should it not have been destroyed by your brother a year ago, when he had the pope under his thumb and our armies at the gates of Rome? Was it not the will of this government that he should take Rome and that pope's reign end by the command of this Republic? Let me quote for you from the order we issued to General Bonaparte nearly one year ago, in which we commanded that he destroy "the centre of unity of the Roman religion, the irreconcilable enemy of the Republic"*.

Talleyrand: The Ambassador cannot answer for his brother, Citizen Director. And I have not yet told him of his brother's role in this next act for the Republic in Italy.

J. Bonaparte: It is true, Citizens, that I cannot speak for my brother's decision to make peace with the papal government a year ago. But know this: only weeks before Duphot's death, my brother sent correspondence to me full of outrage at the papal government for allowing an Austrian general to have command of the papal forces. He instructed me to threaten the very existence of the Papal States if the pope failed to immediately dismiss the Austrian enemy of this government. My brother was prepared to take Rome, justified by its conniving with the enemies of France.†

Director La Revelliere: Justification, Citizen? We need no justification other than that it is right to end a tyranny. So long as there is a pope, there will be signs of political and religious tyranny. So long as there is a pope, this Republic of equality, reason and the new Religion of Man — Theophilanthropy — will be ever under threat, for the pope will never accede to our new ideas and will seek ever to repress and destroy them.

The Republic cannot abide his presence. In the spring, it is our intention to introduce new religious festivals, even a public liturgy that will banish the old ways of the Church entirely

---

* *The Thermidorean Regime and the Directory, 1794–1799* by Denis Woronoff, 1972, quoting at p. 82 an order to Napoleon, dated 3 February 1797, signed by Directors Barras, Reubell and La Revelliere.
† Napoleon so instructed his brother in a letter dated 10 December 1797.

Act II, Scene III   35

from our society.* The people will have their civic instructions from this Religion of Man and of the State, without the need any longer to reference superstition and legend in order to find a moral purpose. Their lives will be ordered to the calendar of the state, not to the calendar of the saints.

And when they see that even the pope himself is finished and that Rome, too, is a republic, they will see that the Christian Church is a dead thing of the past, and embrace a new faith — in the ideals of this Republic!

In any event, the pope's rule was given to him by Frenchmen invading Italy. Charlemagne assured the temporal power of the pope, and the new rulers of France shall revoke it from him. We have directed General Bonaparte to order the armies under the command of General Berthier to take Rome and complete the work of the revolution in Italy.

Talleyrand: Would you care to see a copy of Napoleon's letter to General Berthier, Ambassador? A copy arrived in my possession a few hours ago.

J. Bonaparte: Yes, minister, I should like to see it, indeed! [*Talleyrand hands it to Bonaparte and he reads.*]

> To General Berthier: *The Executive Directory, Citizen General, has seen with the greatest indignation the conduct just taken by the court of Rome towards the ambassador of the French Republic. The murderers of the brave General Duphot will not go unpunished. The intention of the Executive Directory is that you march immediately to Rome, in the greatest secrecy. You will march, as soon as possible and through long days, to Rome.*
>
> *The Cisalpine Republic, being mended with the pope, must take no part in our quarrel with this prince, and*

---

* Woronoff notes that the Directory introduced the calendar and rites of Theophilanthropy in the spring of 1798.

must maintain itself in the most exact neutrality. It will therefore be essential that the Government of the Republic formally declares to the Minister of Pope that he takes no part in the quarrel between France and the pope. It would also be essential that the Cisalpine Republic send a minister as soon as possible to Vienna, who will be especially responsible for declaring that it remains neutral in this quarrel, and that it would only be in the event that some power, which is not likely, wanted to meddle in the quarrel between France and Rome, that she would find herself obliged to take part.

The speed of your march on Rome is of the greatest importance; it alone can ensure the success of the operation. As soon as you have enough troops at Ancona, you will set them in motion. You will secretly promote the meeting of all the countries adjacent to this city, such as the Duchy of Urbino and the province of Macerata.

You will only publish your manifesto against the pope when your troops are at Macerata. You will say in a few words that the only reason you are marching on Rome is the need to punish the assassins of General Duphot and those who have dared to disregard the respect they owe to the French ambassador. The King of Naples will not fail to send you one of his ministers, to whom you will say that the Executive Directory of the French Republic is not led by any view of ambition; that, by the way, if the French Republic was generous enough to stop in Tolentino when she had more serious reasons for complaints against Rome, it would not be impossible that, if the pope gives satisfaction which satisfies the Government, this affair could be ended.

While making these remarks, you will continue to march. The art here consists in gaining a few steps, so that when the King of Naples perceives that your plan is to reach Rome, there is no longer time to stop you.

> When you are two days away from Rome, you will then threaten the pope and all the members of the Government who are guilty of the greatest of all crimes, to inspire terror and to drive them away.
>
> If, as the Directory does not doubt, you arrive in Rome, you will use all your influence to organize a Roman Republic, avoiding however all that, ostensibly, could prove that it is a project of this Government to form that republic. You will take care to arrest the leaders of the assassinations committed on 8 Nivose, including Cardinal Albani, as well as his family, and you will seize their papers and sequester their property.
>
> Within two days, the treaty of alliance will be concluded with the Minister of the Cisalpine Republic. The French divisions which are on its territory must be paid and nourished by it.
>
> Make every effort to give this Republic a great impetus for the organization of its finances. Make it conclude an offensive and defensive treaty of alliance with the Ligurian Republic, so that they oblige each other to procure four or five thousand troops, in case that one or the other has a war.
>
> The Executive Directory knows your zeal and your talents; it does not doubt the success that will follow you in these various works.[*]

Talleyrand: So it is that two brothers made Rome, and two brothers shall unmake it — Romulus and Remus; Joseph and Napoleon. Citizen Directors, we thank you and bid you farewell.

---

[*] From the letter of Napoleon to General Berthier, dated 11 January 1798.

SCENE IV

The Papal Residence at the Quirinal
14 JANUARY 1798

[*As news of the movement of the French armies reaches Rome, the papal government prepares for invasion and disaster. Pius VI meets at his residence with advisers, Cardinal Doria Pamphili, the Cardinal Secretary of State, Cardinal Romualdo Braschi, the "neponte," the pope's nephew, and Cardinal Giulio Maria della Somaglia, the Vicar General of Rome.*]

Pius: No.

Doria: But, Holiness, you must leave Rome. If the French enter the city, they will surely take you prisoner and will perhaps even execute you. Do not make the mistake of King Louis. He delayed and dithered when he should have fled. When at last he tried, he was captured and returned to Paris as a prisoner until his own people sacked his palace and marched him to the guillotine. You can expect no better treatment.

Pius: So you ask me to abandon Rome, to abandon my people and the Church, because you speculate that I may be harmed if I fail to do so?

Braschi: No, Uncle, we do not ask you to abandon the Church, but to guarantee that its Head will live in safety — for the good of the Church. The King of Naples will receive you and give you refuge. You need only to cross our border to the south to escape this danger.

Pius: We are not the "head" of the Church, nephew. Christ is the Head. We are charged as Vicar of His Body. We choose to stay.

Brsachi: Your courage is great, Uncle, but I fear your folly is greater.

Pius: Courage merely to remain in my own residence? Does my election to remain here excel the courage of the man in whose shoes I stand, crucified up-side-down on a hill of refuse? Does it exceed that of all his successors, and my predecessors, before Constantine? None fled before the cruelty of Decius or Diocletian.

If I should flee because I may face tribulation, how should I ever again whisper such names in the Canon: *Linus, Cletus, Clement, Sixtus, Cornelius, Cyprian, Lawrence?*

Did Becket or More run before the abuse of their sovereigns? Did the pope abandon Rome to the Germans in 1527 or cower before the coming of the Turks in 1571?

No, mine must be the prayer of St. Ignatius, Peter's successor at Antioch, as he was force-marched to his death at Rome: *I am the wheat of Christ, ground by teeth of beasts to become pure bread.*

Doria: Then what are we to do, Holiness?

Pius: We will prepare and we will pray. In practical matters, we must be ready to safeguard the interests of the Church and the security of her future governance. We shall compose a new bull that shall command that, on my death, the cardinals immediately elect a successor, even on the same day as my death. The bull will dispense with the usual mourning period. We trust that, at the appropriate time, you will be sure to offer the requiem on behalf of Our soul.[*]

The bull will also waive the formalities of the conclave. Doria, yours will be the greatest charge. You must assemble those members of the Sacred College that are at hand or who can easily reach whatever place of assembly you may determine. Then you must ensure that the College quickly elects my successor and that the news of the election reaches the world

---

[*] Azara notes the plan for a new bull on succession in a letter of 25 January 1798.

Act II, Scene IV 41

without delay. You must crown the new pope triumphantly, so that there will be no question that the Holy Roman Catholic Church has not been, and will not be, suppressed or wrecked, no matter what armies overrun the Eternal City. The Church endures and will triumph!

But for now, the whole city shall pray. The Church provides us with propitious timing, as the great feast of St. Peter's Chair in Rome falls in just four days, on 18 January. There is no feast of the calendar that better stands for the authority of Peter and his successors over this city, an authority willed by God to form the rock upon which He built the Church. So with the rights of Peter now threatened with destruction, the Roman Church must mark this feast with great solemnity, and must keep its vigil with a most devout show of contrition, begging God's mercy upon the Roman people. Every vigil is a time for the violet vesture of penance, but on the evening of 17th January, We desire that the whole city, the clergy, religious and laity, make a most devout, public showing of repentance, and that our prayers for clemency last for seven days.

Ours must now be the spirit of Lent: *Thus saith the Lord: Be converted to Me with all your heart, in fasting and in weeping and in mourning.*[*]

We desire that you, Cardinal Vicar General, arrange for a great procession to take place on the Vigil of the Feast of St. Peter's Chair. We shall lead it Ourself, from Santa Maria in Vallicella, across the Tiber and into Saint Peter's.[†] All the clergy and the people shall attend, and We command that the whole city venerate the sacred images of the *Santo Volto* — the Holy Face of our Lord — the portrait of Our Lady from Santa Maria in Portico and the Chains of St. Peter. We shall grant indulgences to all who participate in the procession and in the solemn days of penitence that shall follow.

---

[*] The first line of the Epistle of the Mass of Ash Wednesday (Joel 2:12).
[†] Santa Maria in Vallicella is referred to as "*La Chiese Nuova.*" It is the principal church entrusted to the Oratorians, located a short distance across the Tiber from the Vatican.

Cardinal Somaglia: I shall compose a decree at once, Your Holiness. It shall be issued by tomorrow, so that all the people, the clergy and the religious, may have time to prepare. It shall be written broadly, with the approval of Your Holiness, such that all who are willing to offer prayers for penance and mercy may receive the spiritual benefits you promise. If the Lord God was willing to spare Sodom for the sake of a few righteous men, let Him hear the prayers of all of Rome, begging His mercy, to spare the Chair of the Prince of the Apostles!

SCENE V

The Residence of Cardinal Somaglia
15 JANUARY 1798

[*On 15 January, Cardinal Somaglia assembles members of the papal guards at his residence and instructs them to post a decree throughout the city.*]

Cardinal Somaglia: This solemn decree must be posted and delivered throughout Rome. You are to take it to every church and every religious house; to the cafes and the buildings. By command of His Holiness, the decree shall be publicized as much as possible. It is your task to see that all of the people know of it, and you are to encourage everyone to assemble for the great procession that will take place on the vigil of the feast, two days from now.

For my part, I shall proclaim it now here to you, that you may know its contents and relate them to all whom you meet:

SACRED INVITATION AND NOTIFICATION[*]

Romans, wise and religious Romans, to the blessed God be faithfully attached, and listen to your sovereign, the visible head of the Catholic Church: in the horrible calamities which we have seen just short time ago because of a singular misadventure, and now fiercely exacerbated by infernal malice, you have received from the common father of the faithful, the Supreme Pontiff reigning, a loving invitation to raise your voices to Heaven in order to obtain shelter from such great ills, and you have obediently obeyed him by rushing to the churches, where a devout three days was celebrated.

---

[*] Author's translation of the text of the original Italian, as memorialized by Duppa in Appendix II of his *Journal*.

Therefore HIS HOLINESS *proposed the great means of the divine word that is so effective for the conversion of the heart, in order to better welcome your prayers before the throne of God, and with your saintly hunger for the food of eternal life, you have constantly and untiringly flooded the twelve great churches of Rome, never weary, ever attentive and modest, to the words of the Sacred Orators, with their mouths full of doctrine, to fill you full of zeal to ever better learn your duties, and to excite you to the horror of sin and to the love of the Christian virtues; among you this is not vain flattery, because many have already practiced the two most secret and faithful companions of prayer, alms-giving and fasting.*

Romans, you have done much with the divine help, although much remains to be done, because you must increase your compunction of heart, constancy in purpose, fervor in prayers, so that a loving defense may be made of the Most High God.

And here is the Holy Father, who invites you to delight in a great eternal act of Religion, in which he decrees that the people are all to prostrate themselves, contrite before the Throne of the Most High, in order to implore His defense and His pity.

It will be your faith, animated by the sight of the sacred objects of Religion, which will be carried by the clergy with devout ceremony, through the public streets to the Basilica of St. Peter, on the day that precedes the Solemnity of the Chair of St. Peter in Rome, and will be exposed on the High Altar to public veneration for several days, so our hearts will turn more confidently to God, and the Heart of God will be filled with the fulness of His mercy.

Our divine savior JESUS CHRIST *is the only propitiator for the sins of the whole world. The* MOST HOLY VIRGIN MARY *is our dear mother, and as the Mother of* GOD, *she is the most powerful Mediatrix of any grace before the* MOST HOLY UNDIVIDED TRINITY. *The Prince of the Apostles St.* PETER *is the Father, the foundation, the glory* of Roman Christianity: these are the subjects to whom are dedicated the august monuments that will be borne in the most solemn procession.

This venerable rite has its origin in the ancient Covenant, we read about in the Second and Third Book of Kings, practiced by David and Solomon; read the Book of Ezra and you will see it fervently requested by all the People in thanksgiving to God for their delivery from slavery in Babylon. I recall finally the famous command given to Joshua by God Himself to lead the Ark in religious procession for seven days around the walls of Jericho.

But in the new covenant of pious customs, can we number the various processions in each of the Catholic Churches, and especially in the Roman Church, the Mother and Teacher of all the others? They repeat themselves more than once a year, and they are always practiced in time of calamities and for the grave needs of the Church and the State. Now what circumstances for us were ever more sorrowful and urgent? And when was there ever a stronger reason to follow in the footsteps of our ancestors? Let us taken them with humility and courage, and do not doubt.

The day selected by HIS HOLINESS is Wednesday 17 January, the Vigil of the Chair of St. Peter, and it shall be a day of fasting, according to the precept for a vigil, for all Secular Clergy and for all Religious Persons of both sexes, so long as they are not legitimately prevented. For laypersons it is not required but is counselled as an appropriate means of Penance.

On the same Wednesday at about the 16th hour, there will be a solemn procession from the Church of Santa Maria in Vallicella to the Vatican Basilica; and it will be composed of all the secular clergy, and the Religious will join in, as in the great procession of Corpus Domini, and they will carry in the sight of everyone the Venerable, Most Ancient and Wonderful Image of the MOST HOLY SAVIOR, which will be joined by the Miraculous Effigy of SANTA MARIA IN PORTICO, and those Venerable CHAINS by which the

Prince of the Apostles suffered his first persecution, moved by the infernal powers and by human malice; and which, as is recounted in the Acts of the Apostles, the Divine Omnipotence instantly dissolved.

But all must be careful to participate in the Procession itself with an interior sentiment of true compunction, not out of curiosity, or with tumult, but with modesty, humility and devotion; participating with a contrite heart in the public Prayers of the Holy Church, which is the purpose for which Procession Festivals are instituted, or reciting privately the Holy Rosary.

Those who do not participate in the Procession will either stay in the Churches or in their own homes join spiritually in the public Orations, reciting for the same purpose the Seven Penitential Psalms, or the third part of the Rosary, during the time when they will hear the bells of all the Churches, which will ring from 7 o'clock until noon, when the Procession is about to be finished. The same bells will be rung the evening before, Tuesday the 16th, from the 6 pm Angelus into the night in order to give a sign of the coming Service.

When the Sacred Monuments arrive at St. Peter's, they will be placed on the Papal Altar, and will remain exposed for at least eight days to public veneration. During those days, the Chapters of the Basilicas and the Colleges will process, according to their order, singing or reciting the Psalms or the Litany of the Saints or the Third part of the Rosary.

With regard to Religious persons of both sexes obligated to perpetual enclosure, and to all others, both laymen and ecclesiastics, and persons restricted to prison, or who, due to any bodily infirmity, or other legitimate impediment, cannot carry out the above-mentioned works, or any similar one, HIS HOLINESS *allows that an approved confessor, or one to be approved after the present publication, may commute the aforesaid with other pious works: and they may be performed at another time, and the confessor may impose upon them such works as they are able to perform.*

Act II, Scene V

Moreover, HIS HOLINESS *exhorts every man of any order who is able frequently to visit in those days the Vatican Basilica, not only with a truly contrite heart, but also with outward signs of humility and penitence, so that all will see that he goes to ask for forgiveness and mercy; women are especially admonished to wear modest clothes, without vanity, in a pleasing way, so as not to more greatly anger the Lord.*

He likewise orders all Superiors of Religious, and of Congregations of both sexes, that they, at this time, offer particular Prayers, Penances and other Devotions to God, both day and night, which as persons especially chosen by God, HIS HOLINESS *hopes will be all the more efficacious for the Holy Church.*

These good works will not remain without Spiritual reward, since HIS HOLINESS, *to all the Faithful, of both sexes, who devoutly participate in the aforementioned Procession, or who, during the days mentioned above, visit the Sacred Monuments at the Basilica of St. Peter and who recite before them the Seven Penitential Psalms, or the Third Part of the Rosary; and who, in addition, on one of the seven days, at their discretion, who give some alms to the Poor, as much as each sees fit, and finally, if they make a confession and take Communion during that time as requested, at a Church of their choosing, praying for the intentions of our Holy Father to the Lord God,* HIS HOLINESS *will grant a Plenary Indulgence, in the form of a Jubilee, with the same faculties granted to the confessors as already granted by the Bull of the 5th of the current month, and lasting through the 2nd of next February.*

In addition, to anyone who in these days visits St. Peter's Basilica and recites before the Sacred Monuments the Oration that begins Ante oculos tuos Domine or in place of it recites the Pater Noster and the Ave Maria ten times, praying as above, HIS HOLINESS *grants for each day the Indulgence of ten years, and up to as many as Forty.*

Moreover, to all those, who in each of the aforesaid days, at the usual time for the ringing of the bells in the evening, or even at another hour that is more convenient for them, kneel down and recite the Seven Penitential Psalms, or the Third Part of the Rosary, as above, HIS HOLINESS *grants for each day an Indulgence of Seven Years, and up to as many of Forty Years, and to those who continue the same devotions for all seven days, he assigns the same Indulgences as may be acquired by visiting the Seven Churches of Rome.*

HIS HOLINESS *grants that each and every one of the aforementioned Indulgences may be applied by way of suffrage to the blessed Souls in Purgatory.*

These are our weapons, O Romans: holy and peaceful arms that do not bring death, but life, and life eternal to those who handle them well, even indeed to those against whom they are deployed — Hi in Curribus & hi Equis, Nos autem in nomine Domini* *— be constant, therefore, in good works and in trust, since God Himself, by the mouth of the Psalmist, makes us take heart with these consoling words:* Invoca me in die tribulationis tuae, eripiam te, et magnificabis me† *— Yes, by calling upon you, O Great God, we can also magnify you with the Royal Prophet —* Quoniam tu precussiti omnes adversantes mihi fine causa, dentes peccatorum contrivisti. Domini est salus et super populum tuum benedictio tua‡ *— And may it be so.*

Given from our usual Residence,
this 15th day of January 1798.

G.M. CARD. VICARIO.

FILIPPO CANONICO LIBERTI SEGRETARIO.

---

* "They [will call upon] chariots and horses; but we upon the name of the Lord." (Ps. 19)

† "Call upon me on the day of your tribulation, and I will spare you, and you will magnify me." (Ps. 49)

‡ "Because you have struck against all my adversaries with a final blow, you have crushed the teeth of sinners. Salvation is of the Lord and your blessing is over your people." (Ps. 3)

SCENE VI

The Headquarters of General Berthier at Civita Castellana
8 FEBRUARY 1798[*]

[*The French Army under General Berthier advances from the north towards Rome. By 8 February, the army has reached the ancient town of Civita Castellana, about 40 miles north of Rome. Here, Berthier summons the Spanish ambassador, Azara, to convey his terms of surrender to the pope. Also present, listening, are Berthier's chief lieutenants, General Cervoni and General Murat, Napoleon's brother-in-law.*]

Berthier: Your Excellency, at last we meet. We have been searching you out for some time now.

Azara: I have been at Tivoli, General, these last weeks. I could no longer endure the distress and tumult in Rome and so I confess I fled the city. I met General Cervoni while on my way back to Rome and, when he told me you wished to see me, I came here immediately.

Berthier: Ambassador, do you know why I am here?

Azara: I am a witness to the events that brought you here, General. I was in the city on night during which General Duphot was tragically killed. I pleaded with Ambassador Bonaparte that same night to remain in Rome and to see the pope — to reconcile before returning to Paris. Instead, you, and your army, are here. Now it seems there will be reconciliation at the point of a bayonet.

---

[*] Based, in general, on the account given by Azara in his *Memorias*.

Berthier: Whether and how there will be reconciliation depends entirely on the papal government. I am not sent here to destroy, but to exact justice against those who caused the death of a French general on French territory. The innocent have nothing to fear from the Republic.

Azara: Then the pope and his ministers may rest assured, because the papal government had nothing whatsoever to do with General Duphot's death. Surely, the Directory knows that his death was an accident that occurred during an anarchic riot. Ambassador Bonaparte himself had tried to calm the crowd before the violence broke out.

Neither the government nor the Roman people are responsible for what happened. If your orders are to bring justice to the guilty, then there is no cause for the pope to fear for his safety and the continuity of his rule, nor for the people to fear the sword or the musket.

Berthier: If the army is able to enter Rome peacefully, and to discharge its mission without resistance, then, as you say, neither the government nor the people will suffer the slightest coercion or violence. But these are the terms to which the pope himself must accede:

The army must not be challenged on its entry into the city; the government must give over those who are directly responsible for General Duphot's death; and the government must further pay an exaction to the Republic in an amount needed to cover the pay of my soldiers for theses last five months on the march. These are the terms of the Republic. If the pope shall agree, there shall be peace and amity between the States of the Church and the French government.

Azara: And what of the Christian Religion? What shall become of it when your men enter Rome?

Act II, Scene VI   51

Berthier: I have no orders with regard to Religion. It shall continue, in complete freedom.

Azara: So Roman Christianity will be permitted to flourish at Rome, but not at Paris? What of the prerogatives of your new Directors, of your Citizen Director Le Revellier, who wish to introduce an entirely new religion as the foundation of the Revolution?

Berthier: What of it? I have already told you, this army is here to enforce justice for a specific crime committed against the French Republic, not to spread our Revolution to the States of the Church. In any event, true Christianity has nothing to fear from this Theophilanthropy, this new religion of the Republic. True Christianity is the basis for the Revolutionary religion and is, therefore, entirely compatible with it.

Azara: Your Republic has been at war with the Christian Religion for a decade. The Revolution tried to supplant the Roman Church with a new Church of the State. Its varying creeds have resulted in the expulsion of the clergy from your borders, the seizure of the lands of the Church, the destruction of the religious houses, the imprisonment of hundreds of priests, who even now are condemned to your penal colonies, and the deaths of so many more. You have waged civil war against those Frenchmen who wished to maintain the Catholic Religion. You have ordered people to worship an idol called "Reason." And now, once more, the Revolution imposes a new creed that, after all that has occurred, you wish to equate to pure Christianity. If this Theophilanthropy is Christianity by another name, then there is no such thing as Christianity.

Berthier: You indict the new with the sins of the old. The Terror, the Convention, Robespierre are finished. You should be pleased that the religion of the new France is the pure distillation of the old religion. Theophilanthropy: the very term simply means "love of God and Man." This is simple Christian virtue.

Azara: And what "god" is it that Man is to love? Is it the same Christ of the Gospel — "*Verbum caro factum est,*" the healer and preacher, who suffered, died, and rose again to expiate the sins of man?

Berthier: You may hold to these so-called doctrines and dogmas, if you like, but the religion of the Revolution has no need for them. Nor, may I say, did the first Christians. Our religion is like theirs. It frees the people from complex and impenetrable formulae; from superstition and resorting to belief in the so-called "miraculous." Its rituals will be communal, bringing the people together in amity to give thanks for civic virtue, equality and freedom, instead of mindless medieval processions, full of superstitious nonsense, or a Mass where a subservient people stands mute and uncomprehending, staring at the back of a priest.

You have nothing to fear from the religion of the Revolution. It is a Christianity, made practical and accessible, turned towards man for the benefit of man, governed not by unintelligible ancient doctrine and a remote, imperious papal king, but by the benevolence of a republican government that exists to foster the people's welfare.

Azara: You would give them Christ without the Cross, a religion created by the state for its own ends. This is a false comfort and a counterfeit faith, and it seems to me that such a faith can never take hold of the heart, even if it may appeal to the heads of some who believe only what they themselves see. Regardless, is it your wish that I now convey these terms to the pope and, in so doing, assure him of your peaceful intentions and respect for the religious liberty of the Roman people?

Berthier: It is my wish, and yes, you may so assure the papal government. But, Ambassador, there is one final point: it is true

Act II, Scene VI

that this army will take no action to dominate the States of the Church. However, it is the moral duty of the French Republic to give support to persons who, acting of their own volition, wish to pursue our ideals of liberty, equality and brotherhood. If the people of Rome rise against the papal government or wish to throw off the shackles of its religion and its despotism, they shall find a friend in this Republic.

Now, go, Ambassador, and report to me the answer of the pope as soon as you are able. We are leaving here tonight, and we shall continue our march to the south. By tomorrow, look for me at Monte Mario, where we plan to erect a headquarters about 5 miles from the walls of the Vatican.

Azara: I will do my best, General, to give you an answer. As you know, I have no official power in these matters. I can only bring them to the pope and his cardinals. But I will give them the assurances you have given to me.

Good night. [*Azar exits*]

Murat [*Holding a letter*]: There was once a great Roman Senator who was determined to destroy a city. He thought the city was Rome's eternal enemy, and that Rome would have no peace while the city existed. So consumed was the senator with the destruction of this city that he became famous for his incessant uttering of three words: *Carthago delenda est. Carthage must be destroyed.*

Berthier: Yes, Murat, and what of it? I know well the life of Cato.

Murat: Then you must know that the Director La Revellier is the Cato of our governing council. In this letter we received tonight, he writes of the pope as Cato spoke of Carthage — that he must be destroyed. He is still furious that my brother-in-law last year refused the order to sack Rome and wipe the papal power from the Earth. And you are not Napoleon, General. I do not think it possible for you to return to Paris without the head of the pope on a platter, for La Revellier is convinced that the destruction of the papacy will lead in turn to the destruction of the Church itself. *Et Ecclesia delenda est.*[*]

Berthier: We have our orders, and I shall carry out the orders just as I promised Azara. But I warned him: If the Romans rise against the pope and the tyranny of the ecclesiastical government, in the name of the Revolution, then it is our duty to give aid to such efforts. We will not act to shield a tyrant who is deposed by his own subjects.

Murat: And what of the religious question?

Berthier: The religion shall change in time with the change of the government. For now, we will remind the people that obedience to the civil authority, in whatever form God wills that it may take, is a Christian duty. Thus, as I told Azara, the Christian Religion shall be preserved. It shall in fact be made manifest by the acquiescence of the people to a republican government, supported by this army — but only, of course, should the people ask for such a revolution themselves.

---

[*] According to Azara in his *Memorias*, La Revellier was in control of the affairs in Italy and sent Murat specific instructions, ordering the deposition of the pope and the destruction of his temporal power, under the belief that the destruction of the papacy would in turn destroy the Church.

SCENE VII
The Vatican
THE EVENING OF 8 FEBRUARY 1798

[*Following his meeting with Berthier, Azara returns to Rome and goes immediately to the Vatican, where he is received in audience by the pope and the Cardinal Secretary of State, Doria. Azara conveys to them Berthier's terms for the surrender of Rome.*]

Pius: *Placebimus.* We shall agree.

Doria: Holiness, how can we trust Berthier? Do you take his word that he comes only to bring those responsible for Duphot's death to justice?

Pius: No. Our trust is not in Berthier, or Bonaparte, or any man. It is in Almighty God, whom we have beseeched to grant us His clemency, and in the words of Christ to Peter: *and the gates of Hell shall not prevail against it.*

Now is a time for the virtue of Prudence. When the general comes into the city, We shall show him every courtesy, and we shall make it plain that neither this government, nor the people of Rome, are in any sense culpable for the death of Duphot. We shall in no way impede Berthier in his quest to bring to justice the individuals who are, in fact, responsible for the tragic death of his colleague.

Azara: The Revolution and justice cannot go together, Your Holiness.[*]

---

[*] Azara recounts in his *Memorias* that he made this remark to the pope when he presented Berthier's terms.

Pius: The foundation of justice is Truth, Ambassador. And Christ is the Truth. Any government, any system, any philosophy that denies this fact denies the Truth, and, therefore, by definition, will be unable to secure justice. The Revolution denies Christ, and is, thus, by its nature, unjust.

But while Christ is the Truth, Berthier is not the Revolution. God willing, we shall endure his stay, pay his price and let him leave the city and the Church in peace. It is the supreme task of the Roman Pontiff to preserve the Faith, as handed down, and to secure its transmission via the Apostolic Succession. If the pope and the Church and the States of the Church must bow in humility before this man in order to discharge this duty, so we shall. Christ was born in a barn and died on a Cross. Humiliation is only imitation of Him.

Doria, now go and set your signature upon a document that, with Our full authority, grants General Berthier the right to enter Rome, on the terms he has proffered to Us. And then you are to issue a general admonition to Our people, Our beloved Romans, instructing them in the most clear terms that they must accept the entrance of the French into the city, without any resistance. We must place our confidence in Almighty God that, if clergy and people humbly acquiesce in this occupation, these invaders will take the material goods they wish, and leave here, with our spiritual treasures untouched.

SCENE VIII

At the Vatican

THE MORNING OF 9 FEBRUARY 1798

[*Having accepted Berthier's terms of surrender, pursuant to the order of the pope, Doria proclaimed the following decree to the Roman people from St. Peter's, and directed its distribution throughout the city:*]*

> His Holiness, always intent, and always anxious for the quiet and safety of his most beloved subjects, cannot refrain to open to them his paternal heart, upon an occasion, in which their quiet and security might be agitated and disturbed. Romans, wise and virtuous Romans, it is your most beloved sovereign and father, that through our means speaks to you. He informs you that the French army is now approaching this capital, and at the same time is assured that they are not coming with any hostile intentions against you. Therefore, fear nothing, be tranquil, and console yourselves in his presence. He is full of faith in the rectitude and generosity of the Republic, in the moderation and prudent conduct of her generals; thus, fearing nothing himself, and animated by the most tender affection for you, he will not abandon you, and he is confident he never can, in any occasion in which he could perceive you in any way exposed to danger. Your sovereign and father, we repeat it, the head of the Church, gives to you, as must be manifest to you, a new and signal proof of his affection; but at the same time he cannot neglect reminding you of your duty. Your duty is to adapt your faith to that of His Holiness, and even to avoid every occasion in which it could be possible to suspect to the contrary. You must not only not give the least

---

* As memorialized and translated by Duppa in his *Journal*.

offense, in word or deed, to any individual of the French nation, whether he be military or private, as to the individuals of every other nation; but show them every mark of urbanity, and let it be seen in your deportment; and give to them a confirmation of the harmony and friendship that the Holy Father maintains, and is desirous of maintaining, towards the republic. Romans, know you, and know it for your certain guide, that upon such deportment, principally, depends your peace and security.

To that end our Lord employs all the means in his power: but in your attachment to the country, in the love that you ought to have towards yourselves, and towards your families, and in the docility to conform to his wishes, he confides still more.

His Holiness is willing to flatter himself that he shall obtain this obedience by your affection, and by your knowledge of its importance, rather than by fear: but such are the present circumstances, that if any person or persons not mindful of his proper duty, and ungrateful to His Holiness' beneficence, should so far forget himself as to offend, in whatever manner, any individual of the French nation, and forget the name of a Roman, by disregarding the laws of hospitality, or does in any manner disturb that public quiet, he shall not be able otherwise to consider him, than as traitor to the state, subject to the penalty of death.

Ordered likewise, and commanded by His Holiness, that neither in the public squares, nor in the streets, nor in the coffee-houses, nor in the public-houses, you crowd together in groups, nor talk about the present affairs; under pain of being punished as transgressors, according to existing laws already published.

In a word, assure yourselves that His Holiness exerts the most efficacious means to adjust the present differences, therefore we earnestly exhort you to remain peaceable in your respective occupations, and rely on the true love of the best of sovereigns.

Act II, Scene VIII

And the present edict is posted and published in the usual places of Rome, and is binding and obligatory on each person, as much as if he were personally presented with it.

Dated the Chambers of the Vatican,
this 9th day of February, 1798.

G. CARD. DORIA PAMPHILI.

SCENE IX

At the Vatican

10 FEBRUARY 1798*

[*As agreed, on the morning of 10 February 1798, the French Army, under the command of General Cervoni, entered Rome and took possession of the fortress Castle Sant'Angelo that protects the entrance to the Vatican. Accompanied by Azara, Cervoni is sent as ambassador to the pope to set forth formally the reasons for the French invasion. Pius receives him at St. Peter's.*]

Azara: Your Holiness, may I present General Cervoni of the French Army. He is appointed commander of the French troops inside the City of Rome and as representative of his government to the Holy See.

Pius: We cordially receive and welcome you, General.

Cervoni: Your Holiness, it is my duty to solemnly protest to you in the name of the French Directory against the death of General Duphot, shot and killed on sovereign French soil within the States of the Church. It is to exact justice from your government for this crime that we have come.

Pius: We are aware of your purpose here, General, as We have already agreed to permit your army to enter Rome without the slightest resistance so that you may carry out your stated mission. And We know that is only for this reason you have come, and, you shall find that We shall cooperate with you in order that you might accomplish your purpose and then return your men to their homes as quickly as possible.

---

* The following is based upon Azara's account in his *Memorias*.

Cervoni: And Your Holiness shall find that we shall move swiftly. I am commanded to inform you that your sovereignty over the States of the Church will suffer no impairment, nor will we in any way interfere with the practice of the Catholic religion, nor will we seek to take property from any individual.

Today, General Berthier has commanded that this order be posted throughout the city:

> All the inhabitants of the ecclesiastical state can be assured of the protection of the French army, towards worship, the temples, the people & properties.
>
> The faith will be religiously respected, therefore all public demonstrations of worship must continue without any alteration or change.[*]

Our purpose is justice, and, to that end, in order to keep the peace while we are in the city, I propose that, while we are here, we compose the patrols that usually make the rounds of the city with half Roman and half French soldiers, so as to assure the people that our governments are working in concert.

Pius: As you wish, General.

Cervoni: Moreover, we have no wish to disturb Your Holiness' household. You are free to retain your usual guard, and to carry out all of your regular functions, both sacred and profane, just as if there were not a single French soldier in Rome.

Pius: Yes, General, We are, of course, agreeable to such an arrangement, and We thank you for your courtesy. Is there anything else you wish to convey to Us now?

---

[*] Author's translation of Berthier's order from the French as memorialized by Duppa in his *Journal*.

Act II, Scene IX 63

Cervoni: No, Your Holiness. As I said, we have come to punish the wrong-doers, not to attack the Roman people or to harass the Holy See. So if you will excuse me, I must be about the business that brings us here. Good morning, Your Holiness. [*Exit Cervoni*].

Pius: Well, Azara, perhaps the faith that is size of mustard seed has moved a mountain. Perhaps God in His mercy has answered us, and these men will take what they must and leave us in peace.

Azara: If they do, Your Holiness, it would be the meekest act yet of the Revolution.

Pius: Ah, but Grace knows no bounds, Azara. It can penetrate even the hardest of hearts. *Nothing shall be impossible for God.*

Azara: Then may it be done to Rome according to your word. I take my leave, Your Holiness, now to return to General Berthier so that I may ensure that Grace has, in fact, penetrated.

SCENE X

General Berthier's Camp at Mount Mario, Outside Rome
11 FEBRUARY 1798[*]

[*Following the meeting between the pope and General Cervoni, Azara travels to the French headquarters on Mount Mario outside of Rome in the hope of reaching a binding plan to govern the activities of the French while they occupy Rome and to ensure that they adhere to their pronouncements regarding the sovereignty of the pope and the freedom of Religion.*]

Berthier: Greetings, Ambassador, I am pleased you have come. Now that our men have secured the city, there is much to discuss and your services will be required.

Azara: To the contrary, General, I thought most of our work was already accomplished. As you say, your men entered the city peacefully. I was present at the meeting between the pope and General Cervoni yesterday, where they agreed to work cooperatively for the security of the city. Cervoni read your order ensuring the security of the people, and the freedom of Religion. His Holiness received it all with great serenity, and assured Cervoni that the papal government shall not impede you in your mission to punish those responsible for the death of General Duphot. Having accomplished as much already, we now need only to plan for the exact manner in which Duphot's killers will be brought to justice, after which, of course, the army will withdraw from Rome.

Berthier: Certainly, yes, the objective of the French government remains the punishment of the perpetrators of Duphot's murder. But, as you will no doubt agree, since the general was killed

---

[*] The following is based upon Azara's account in his *Memorias*.

amongst a riot of the pope's soldiers, and killed on sovereign French territory, we have no choice but to hold the papal government responsible in some measure for this crime.

Azara: I am afraid I do not understand, General. Only yesterday General Cervoni spoke of cooperation with the papal government, and the pope acquiesced. It was agreed that individuals, not the States of the Church, must answer for Duphot's death.

Berthier: You are confused, Ambassador. There is no distinction between the state and the individual in this case. General Duphot was a representative of the Directory, not merely some private person. We are here on behalf of one government to exact justice from another. The Church fancies itself a state and, thus, it is liable for punishment accordingly. I have already drawn the precise terms we demand, and you shall carry them to the pope and his government forthwith. And the terms are as follows:

> The indemnity set in 1797 by the Treaty of Tolentino shall be increased from 15 million livres to 20 million livres, payable immediately.
> The papal government shall supply the French army with enough fresh horses to allow the army to return to Paris.
> The papal government shall arrest and execute the individuals responsible for General Duphot's death.
> The papal government shall erect a pyramid at St. Peter's with an inscription detailing the heroic death of General Duphot at the hands of criminals.
> And the papal government shall dispatch the Cardinal Nephew, and several Roman nobles, to Paris, where they shall, in public audience before the Directory, request pardon for murder of General Duphot.
> If the papal government agrees and complies, the French army shall withdraw as promised.

Act II, Scene X

Azara: General, I cannot convey these terms to the pope! I am the ambassador of the Spanish Crown, not messenger of the Directory, and I refuse to put before His Holiness such terrible demands as these, especially as I was present when General Cervoni offered only mild and cooperative terms yesterday. I am sorry, General, but I must refuse.

Berthier: Ambassador, you are as much in the power of the French Army as the lowliest Roman whose street we now occupy. We have the same authority to direct your actions as we have to decide whether any Roman may attend to his labors or any simple priest may pray his Mass. Do not mistake your position under the rule of the French Directory — and do not think that the Directory is not in full control of this city and of the Ecclesial State. We shall dispose of it as we see fit, not only for its crimes against Duphot, but for its hatred of the free French Republic!

Azara: Then your words mean nothing, General, for but a moment ago, you promised that you had come only for one, limited purpose. But in the next moment, you reveal yourself as our very own Sulla, marching on Rome and ruling it with the absolute authority of a Dictator. How you fancy yourself a Republican, when, like Sulla before you, your actions destroy liberty, is a greater mystery than any of the mysteries of Religion.

I am a friend to the pope, and I must live here among the Romans. How would you have me present such oppressive and offensive terms to them?

Berthier: My dear Azara, whether you speak these terms, or another tells them to the pope, they will be told to him. And he will accept them, or he will surely be the last of his line — and I trust you know that the end of this institution would be a great cause of rejoicing at Paris and might even earn me the accolades given to Sulla, to whom you design to compare me. But, if you wish that the words come from the mouths of others,

I shall simply send with you Cervoni and my own brother, who is here as my aide, and they will speak the words to the pope that you refuse to utter. I will summon them here, and you will take them to the Vatican and the matter shall be closed.

Azara: I am then to stay the night here and return with these men tomorrow?

Berthier: Not all, Ambassador! I have no wish to inconvenience you further.

Azara: Thank you general. Good night.

Berthier: Yes, good night. You shall leave for the Vatican now. I will send for my brother and Cervoni to join you on the way.

Azara: General, it is after nine o'clock already!

Berthier: Then hurry you must, Ambassador. Do not keep the pope waiting. I am sure he will be eager to hear the final terms to which he is subject.

SCENE XI

At the Vatican

JUST BEFORE MIDNIGHT, 11 FEBRUARY 1798

[*With great reluctance, Azara returns to the Vatican with Generals Cervoni and Berthier, to present the latest terms of surrender to the pope. They are there met by Cardinal Doria Pamphili.*]

Doria: Gentlemen, what is the meaning of your coming here at this hour? What has happened?

Azara: Your Eminence, I was summoned to General Berthier's camp this evening. I am here at his insistence to deliver to the pope certain terms regarding the matter of the French occupation of the city.

Doria: Perhaps I am tired at this hour and am thus confused, Ambassador. His Holiness permitted the French army to enter the city yesterday, with no resistance, following his meeting with General Cervoni, with whom he reached clear terms. Is it not so, General?

Cervoni: It is true that I met the pope yesterday and that he acquiesced to the terms I presented.

Doria: Then what is it that brings you here, a foreign ambassador and two generals of a foreign army at the Tomb of the Apostle, less than an hour before midnight with such urgency?

Azara: It seems, Your Eminence, that the terms conveyed to the pope were merely partial; only an hour ago, in the presence of these men, General Berthier promulgated this document, setting down additional terms with which the French demand compliance. I am its unwilling messenger. [*hands to Doria*]

Doria [*reading*]: Is it, in truth, the purpose of the Directory to humiliate His Holiness? You demand modification of the Treaty of Tolentino, so punishing to the Church, after only a year's time?

Azara: They demand modification to their prior terms of surrender after only a day's time, Cardinal.

Cervoni: Cardinal, our men are already within your walls. Even as we speak, they command the heights of the Castle Sant'Angelo. An order from General Berthier can bring those men from the Castle to the very foot of the papal altar in a matter of minutes. These are the terms, and there is the place for your signature.

Doria: And at the foot of the same altar we pray, "*Iudica me Deus, and discerne causam meam de gente non sancta: ab homine iniquo et doloso erue me*".* It is not for me to decide these terms, but to pray this prayer of deliverance from such an iniquitous regime as is here present. I am the minister to His Holiness, the sovereign of Rome. To him I shall present this document.

Cervoni: Do what you must quickly.

Doria: Words spoken to another traitor. I shall return with an answer.

---

* "Judge me O God, and distinguish my cause from an unholy nation; from the unjust and deceitful man deliver me." The first verse of the Preparatory Prayers "at the foot of the altar," recited by the priest at the beginning of the Traditional Mass.

SCENE XII

Doria and the Pope

MIDNIGHT, 12 FEBRUARY 1798

Pius: Was I wrong, Doria, to trust them? Am I like Priam, a foolish king who has opened the gates to receive his enemy, though mine was not hidden as was Priam's?

Doria: No, Holiness, you discharged your duty to your subjects, to preserve the peace in the face of monstrous aggression. If you are Priam, you are Priam without a Hector to withstand the Achilles that is now within our walls.

Pius: Resistance would now cause only the useless shedding of blood, I am afraid, and would provide at long last the excuse to ban Religion. Can you imagine, Doria, Religion itself put under a counterfeit interdict in the city of Peter and Paul?

Doria: Can you imagine a statute to an idol erected at the altar of Notre-Dame in Paris? And yet it was done in the name of the Revolution. This so-called "ideology" that has infected these men knows no limit to its passion for the destruction of the Christian order.

Pius: Then you have your answer, Cardinal. Our most solemn duty is the protection of the Faith and its transmission. To allow a break in the chain is not permissible. No amount of gold, nor horses, nor the erection of monuments, nor the groveling of clerics before an impious government obviates our duty. The Faith is the pearl of great price; whatever the cost of its preservation is no cost at all. We therefore charge you, as Cardinal Secretary of State, to execute their treaty on Our full authority.

Doria: *Domine, exaudi orationem meam.*

Pius: *Et clamor meus ad te veniat.**

---

* Taken from the Psalms, this antiphon (Lord, hear my prayer) and response (And let my cry come unto Thee) is a common liturgical prayer that is also part of the priest's preparatory prayers at the beginning of the Traditional Mass.

SCENE XIII

The French at the Roman Forum and the Pope at St. Peter's
15 FEBRUARY 1798

> *With the approbation of the pope, Doria executes the treaty as demanded by the French before dawn on 13 February 1798. Two days later, on the 23rd anniversary of Pius' election as pope, Berthier himself enters Rome in triumph. He precedes to the Capitol area, the site of the ancient Roman Forum, to address the people of the city. There, with the French army assembled around him, replete with guns and mortars, Berthier speaks to a large crowd, many of whom were revolutionaries placed there by the French in advance.*
>
> *At the same hour, 10 a.m., the pope assembles at St. Peter's with the clerical government, the cardinals and prelates, to sing the* Te Deum *in thanksgiving for the anniversary of his coronation.*

Berthier (at the Roman Forum): Shades of Cato, of Pompey, of Brutus, of Cicero, of Hortensius, receive the homage of free Frenchmen on that capitol, where you have so often defended the rights of the people, dignified the Roman Republic.

With the olive of peace come there Gallic sons, to reestablish on the same place the altars of liberty that were originally raised by the first Brutus.

And you, Roman people, in reacquiring your legitimate rights, you already feel what blood it is that flows in your veins, and you have only to cast your eyes around you, to see those monuments of glory that represent the ancient grandeur and virtue of your fathers.*

Now, therefore, by the authority given me by the French Republic, I hereby publish the following decree, abolishing

---
* Berthier's very words, as recorded by Duppa in his *Journal*.

henceforth the temporal power of the pope and restoring to you, the Roman people, a free Republic as of old:

> *The Roman people are now again entered into the rights of sovereignty, declaring their independence, possessing the government of ancient Rome, constituting a Roman republic. The general in chief of the French army in Italy declares, in the name of the French republic, that he acknowledges the Roman republic independent, and that the same is under the special protection of the French army.*
>
> *The general in chief of the army acknowledges, in the name of the French republic, the provisional government which has been proposed by the sovereign people.*
>
> *In consequence, every temporal authority emanating from the old government of the Pope, is suppressed, and shall no more exercise any function.*
>
> *The general in chief will make all the dispositions necessary to secure the Roman people their independence. In order, therefore, that the government may be well arranged, and that the new laws be founded upon the basis of liberty and equality, he will take all the necessary measures to secure the happiness of the Roman people.*
>
> *The French general, Cervoni, is charged with taking care of the police, and the safety of the city of Rome, as also to install the new government.*
>
> *The Roman republic, acknowledged by the French republic, encompasses all the country that remained under the temporal authority of the Pope, after the treaty of Campo Formio.*
>
> ALEXANDER BERTHIER.
>
> ROME, *the 15th of February, 1798; the first year of liberty, proclaimed in the Roman forum, and ratified on the capitol, with free voice, and subscribed to by innumerable citizens.*[*]

---

[*] As memorialized by Duppa in his *Journal*.

Act II, Scene XIII   75

    Now, what say you, free citizens of a free republic?

* * *

[*At the very hour Berthier declares the end of papal rule, the pope, in the Sistine Chapel, addresses the papal government.*]

Pius: Venerable Brethren, it is with great joy that We join with you today to thank Almighty God for Our election as Vicar of Christ and sovereign of Rome. Amid the present dangers that threaten Our rights, as given by God, and the violence that seeks to suppress and supplant the Faith, may we persevere in our duties according to the courage of the Holy Martyrs, that each shall follow Christ to the end.

    On this anniversary of Our coronation, We solemnly declare that We shall never cede to any power the patrimony of St. Peter, given in trust to Our governance for the purpose of the perpetuation of the Christian Faith. What may be given, shall be given, if necessary. That which cannot be given, shall not be given, for, as the Apostle tells us, no power in heaven, or on earth, or under the earth, shall separate us from the love of Christ.

    The sovereign pontiff rules in the name of Christ, and wears this crown not for his own glory, but for the praise and glory of the Holy Trinity. And thus, regardless of misfortunates and the snares of our enemies, let us sing out the ancient hymn of thanksgiving to Almighty God, from whom all power and authority on earth originates.

[*The pope intones the* Te Deum.]

> *Te Deum laudámus: te Dominum confitémur.*
>   *Te ætérnum Patrem omnis terra venerátur.*
> *Tibi omnes Angeli; tibi cœli et univérsae potestátes.*
>   *Tibi Chérubim et Séraphim incessábili voce proclámant:*
> *Pleni sunt cœli et terra majestátis glóriæ tuæ.*
> *Te gloriósus Apostolórum chorus;*

Te Prophetárum laudábilis númerus;
Te Mártyrum candidátus laudat exércitus.
Te per orbem terrárum sancta confitétur Ecclésia:
Patrem imménsæ majestátis;
Venerándum tuum verum et únicum Fílium;
Sanctum quoque Paráclitum Spíritum.
Tu Rex glóriæ, Christe. Tu Patris sempitérnus es Fílius.
Tu ad liberándum susceptúrus hóminem, non horruísti
Vírginis úterum.
Tu, devícto mortis acúleo, aperuísti credéntibus regna
cælórum.
Tu ad déxteram Dei sedes, in glória Patris. Judex créderis
esse ventúrus.
Te ergo quǽsumus, tuis fámulis súbveni, quos pretióso
sánguine redemísti.
Ætérna fac cum sanctis tuis in glória numerári.*

* * *

[*While the pope, cardinals and prelates of the papal government sing the* Te Deum, *across the Tiber at the Forum, the French, working with Romans who wish to bring the Revolution to Italy, call out for the deposition of the pope. A Roman lawyer and French partisan by the name of Riganti climbs upon a table set up in the middle of the Forum, while armed French troops ensure that only the revolutionaries may speak among the crowd.*]

Riganti: Roman people, do you want to throw off the yoke that oppresses you and recover your old freedom and mode of government?

Shouts from the Crowd Surrounding the Speaker's Table [*all placed there by the revolutionaries and French conspirators*]: We want to be free!

---

* The *Te Deum* is an ancient hymn of thanksgiving used to praise God on momentous occasions and major feasts.

Act II, Scene XIII

Riganti: You will be free! And do you wish to re-establish your former Roman consuls?

Shouts from the Crowd: We want it so! We want it so!

Riganti: I have here in my hand the names of five men, whom I propose we make our new consuls — not two as in the days of Cicero, but five, just as five directors govern our liberator and sister state, the French Republic. Will you take, Romans, as your consuls, your fellow citizens Constantini, Persuti, Barsi, Bonelli and me, Riganti? Raise your voices!

Shouts from the Crowd [*again, only those closest to the Speaker's table*]: Here, here! Here, here! We acclaim them the consuls of the Roman republic!

Rignati: Now, then, let us go through the city and proclaim to every citizen his new freedom, the glory of our new republic!

Shouts from the Crowd: Freedom! Freedom! Long live the Roman republic! Long live the French republic!*

---

* The description of the behavior of the crowd, and names of the consuls, are recounted in Azara's *Memorias*.

SCENE XIV

At the Vatican

THE EVENING OF 15 FEBRUARY 1798

[*On the evening of the anniversary of the pope's coronation, 15 February, 1798, Cervoni, accompanied by another French General, Haller, and their troops, entered the Vatican to formally inform the pope of his deposition and the foundation of the new Roman Republic. The French enter Pius' private rooms where he greets the generals and their men.*]

Pius: Have you come out, as against a robber, with your armed soldiers, to find Us, General? Was it not a mere five days past that We met you here, and agreed to all that you asked of Us to secure justice for the unfortunate General Duphot? Why come you here now with these men under arms?

Cervoni: I am here, Holy Father, not only as the general in charge of the city, but also as the messenger of your own people. General Bethier has stated since we came here that we came to exact justice for the murder of General Duphot. But, as representatives of a free republic, General Berthier cautioned that this army will not resist the wishes, should they be expressed by the Roman people, to become a free and equal people, governing themselves as do the French across the Alps.

Today, in your own ancient capital, the people of Rome rose up, of their own volition, and have proclaimed a republic this very day. We are in their service now, as much as we are in the service of the free French Republic. Thus, it falls to me to inform Your Holiness that your temporal reign over Rome and the other lands of the so-called Papal States is at an end, and you will forthwith execute a declaration renouncing your civil power [*handing the pope a Declaration*]

Nonetheless, the person of Your Holiness shall not be harmed and you may continue to exercise your spiritual functions as Bishop of Rome. General Haller has in his hand a decree I have signed calling for the people to give thanks on this coming Sunday at a Solemn Mass for the foundation of the new Roman Republic. So you shall see, Holy Father, that we have no wish to suppress Religion. Yet we cannot resist the will of the people to be free.

Haller, read the proclamation to His Holiness.

Haller [*stepping forward, reads*]:

> *The foundation of political liberty rests on the exact observation of religion and the law, on which, in a peculiar manner depends the protection of a free people. In evidence of which truth the sovereign people makes it known, that tomorrow, at a convenient hour, will be sung a solemn mass at the altar of the tribune of the august temple of the Vatican, with the joyful voice of the* Te Deum. *Therefore, the devout and free Roman people are invited to attend, and thank, with a glad heart, the Most High, who is the Supreme Author of religion and liberty.**

Pius: Do you know, General, that this very morning, We gathered with Our Court to sing the *Te Deum* in thanksgiving for Our coronation as sovereign pontiff? Now you have decreed that, in the name of my own people, there shall be sung the same hymn to thank God for Our deposition.

You wish to offer the Mass, proclaiming the deposition of the Roman pontiff, at an altar over which reads the mandate of the successors of Peter: *O Pastor Ecclesiae, tu omnes Christi pascis agnos et oves.*† Are you the new pastors of the flock of the Lord?

---

* As recorded by Duppa in his *Journal,* wherein he notes that the referenced Sunday was, that year, Quinquagesima Sunday, the Sunday before Ash Wednesday.
† The Latin inscription around the base of the dome in St. Peter's, over the Papal Altar: "O Shepherd of the Church, you feed all the lambs and sheep of Christ."

Act II, Scene XIV   81

Haller: You thanked God for your own power. The people thank Him for the end of it!

Pius: You have as much right to take the temporal power from the Chair of Peter as did Pilate to condemn Our Lord to the Cross. You would have no power here were it not given to you by the point of a bayonet. You bring a strange sort of liberty, rather like Flaminius proclaiming the freedom of the Greeks. We shall not sign any renunciation of the temporal rights of the Roman Pontiff, as We may not impair the rights of Our successors, who are the heirs of Peter.[*]

Cervoni: Your Holiness has seen reason at every stage to this point. Do not change course at this late hour. By signing the renunciation, you do no harm to your spiritual functions, nor do you diminish those same prerogatives on behalf of your successors. Have I not just shown you that, with my sanction, the first act of the Roman Republic shall be the public celebration of a Solemn Mass at St. Peter's?

Pius: You have shown Us that you will use Religion to take hold of the heart of the Church. Was it not said in Paris 10 years ago that a new Gallican Church — your so-called Constitutional Church — would save and purify Christianity for a liberated people?

Haller: Has it failed to do so? The Gallican Church is alive. Its priests and bishops are chosen by the people. It promotes civic peace, harmony with the modern order of the state. It promotes a French rite of the Mass, said in French, as it is a French Church for the French people — living under the creed of Liberty, Equality and Fraternity. You loathe it only

---

[*] Duppa reports Pius' concern for his successors as his reason for refusing to sign the declaration.

because it rejects your false claims of power to rule over a national church from your imperial throne.

Pius: Is your creed the Credo of the Apostles? Can unity with the Roman Pontiff, successor of Peter, be hateful to true Christians, to the true Church? No. Your Revolution has cut off many heads, not the least of which is the true head and guarantor of universal unity of the Church, the Bishop of Rome. The Gallican Church has traded its rightful master for the false master of the state that now dominates it and forces upon it all manner of novelties in belief and practice.

And, in time, the errors and falsehoods and lunatic creeds that are the true tyrants of France will smash the Constitutional Church with the same force with which they tried to smash every priest and bishop who would not swear the false oath!

Cervoni: No, Your Holiness, the Republic and the Church of France co-exist, side-by-side. It will be the same here, with the sister Roman Republic.

Pius: Side by side they may be, General. Is it not true, as We hear, that at the Cathedral of Paris, the great altar is given over to celebration of the hideous cult of Theophilanthropy, so beloved by your Directory, while the priests are consigned to a side altar at which they may only offer Holy Mass when doing so does not interfere with the worship of the government's idols?

Haller: This is intolerable, General! This man is a zealot who cares only for the preservation of his irrational and out-of-date customs. The people want liberty, yet we banter with this irrelevant old fool who insults the Revolution that has freed the people — and the Church — from his shackles. Enough! Sign the renunciation or we shall throw you into the tower where you may rot. Perhaps better we should deport you to Guinea where you can end your days laboring by the side of your beloved priests who refused the oath!

Act II, Scene XIV   83

Cervoni [*handing Pius the Declaration*]: Sign, and we shall go. [*Haller and the soldiers step forward*]

Pius [*taking the Declaration to his desk he writes*]: We cede Our authority to force. Pius the Sixth.* We can do nothing other than acquiesce before the inscrutable designs of Divine Providence.† Take it, General.

Haller [*taking the Declaration*]: We shall take this, and more. Get up, Holy Father. You no longer have need for this desk, nor chair, nor any of the fine furniture in this room. These are the trappings of prince. You are now a simple priest. Let us assist you in your humility.

[*to his men*] Remove every piece of furniture in these rooms immediately. If the pope wishes to remain in this city, he shall live in the manner of the common citizen. Good evening, Citizen Brachi! [*the soldiers proceed to take the furniture, also removing the pope's breviary and a tobacco box*]‡

Pius: You take from an old man, whom you address now as "citizen", his two little consolations — his breviary and an old tobacco box. Even these small cruelties you will not overlook.

Haller: We are not here to overlook a thing. We are here to carry out the will of the Roman people. Take the book, the box, the desk, the chair and whatsoever else is here.

Pius: Cervoni, do you know the Introit that will be prayed at your Solemn Mass this Sunday, the last before Lent?

Cervoni: It is long since I have read the Missal, Your Holiness.

---

* Duppa records these words as accompanying Pius' signature on the renunciation.
† Ludwig Pastor, in his life of Pius VI, attributes these words to the pope at the moment of the renunciation.
‡ Azara, Duppa and Pastor all described the French as removing all of the pope's furniture and possessions.

Pius: Esto mihi in Deum protectorem, et in locum refugii, ut salvum me facias: quoniam firmamentum meum et refugium meum es tu: et propter nomen tuum dux mihi eris, et enutries me. Let there be for me protection in God, and a place of refuge, so that you may save me: for you are my foundation and refuge: and you lead me according to your name, and you will nourish me.

You may take these things from me, but the place of refuge you cannot confiscate. Take what you will, and go.

Haller: I am afraid it is you who should go, sir. General, it is my counsel that we remove this man from Rome. He may go to Tuscany. We shall provide him an escort and some means on which to live. Let him take his precious cardinals with him. But, let him go forth from this city as an exile and let him go now.

Pius: We have given you the renunciation of power and still you take from Us the smallest possession, even a chair and a desk. These things mean nothing to Us. You may do with Us what you wish. We shall not quit Rome. We shall neither leave Rome, nor the Church.

Cervoni: Enough. Your fate, Holy Father, is in the hands of the new Roman government. For now, this army shall not touch your person. General Haller, have your men secure the Vatican and leave a guard here. His Holiness shall be confined to his rooms. Good night, Your Holiness.

SCENE XV

Azara's Apartments
16 FEBRUARY 1798[*]

[*On the day following the pope's forced renunciation of his temporal power, the French generals, Berthier, Cervoni and Haller, convene a meeting at the apartments of the Spanish ambassador, Azara. Joining the generals are the newly-minted "consuls" of the Roman Republic, who now purport to represent the government of the new state.*]

Cervoni: Good day, Ambassador. Thank you for agreeing to see us.

Azara: It is my duty, as the representative of the Spanish crown, to receive you as the present ruling powers. And I wish to personally thank you for posting extra guards around my apartments.

Haller: Did the celebrations at the Liberty Tree just planted under your windows alarm you, Ambassador?

Azara: Lawlessness alarms me, General Haller. I wish to do my duties here. I do not wish to become another head chopped in the name of "liberty." Thus, again, I thank you for your protection of my safety.

Berthier: Ambassador, we have trusted your good work since we arrived here, and you have done as the French Republic has asked. You conveyed our terms to the former government and you have assisted us to maintain peace here, as was and is our desire. I told you that we came to exact justice for the murder

---

[*] This account is taken from Azara's *Memorias*, wherein he describes the conduct of the French in the city, the vandalism of the churches and his meeting with the new "consuls" who wish to see the pope removed from Italy.

of General Duphot, and this remains our purpose. I also told you that, if the Roman people rose up in the name of their own freedom against the papal government, we, as representatives of a free republic, would support their desires, because it is our moral duty to do so. I have remained true to my word, both to you, and to those who have now removed the papal government and founded their own republic. So our mission is now a dual one — to prosecute the murders of General Duphot and to assist the new republican government to ensure the liberty and equality of its people, rights so long denied them.

Azara: Do you carry out these purposes now by allowing your men to run wild in Rome? In the last days, I have seen Roman nobles wandering the streets, having been put out of their homes where your officers now quarter themselves in great luxury. It seems to me that you have sent soldiers to nearly every public building in Rome, every church certainly, to deface and remove the papal coats of arms. The city is impassible due to these soldiers, busying themselves with vandalism, blocking the way as they smash the symbols of the papacy.

Haller: This is the work of the Roman Republic, restored from its ancient glory. Why, these men here are the consuls, successors of Brutus and Cato and Cicero. So they now employ that tool of their forefathers, *damnatio memorae*, to blot out the memory of despots. This is a Roman act and an ancient one, not an invention of the Revolution, as you suggest.

Azara: By whatever name you call it, it is the obliteration of civilization — that is, of history and Religion, which, together, constitute civilization.

Berthier: And that brings us to why we are here. The Rome of two days ago is now as old as the Rome of Romulus. In cooperation with the new government, the Directory in Paris has sent orders that we undertake every effort to firmly and

Act II, Scene XV

permanently establish the consuls in authority and remove any question as to their legitimacy. To this end, the Directory has decreed that the pope must be expelled from Rome. His presence here, as the embodiment of a dead order, is an impediment to securing the rights of the Republic. The Directory has commanded that we inform you, due to your special relationship with the former government, before we officially direct the removal of the pope.

Azara: Last night my secretary was admitted to see the pope. He reported to me this morning that your army has deprived the man of his most meager belongings, even a desk and a chair. I am told he wept before my secretary for lack of his breviary, which your men took from him, so that he cannot even pray the Office, as he is commanded as a priest.

And, yet again, only yesterday you were heard to promise that His Holiness, although deprived of his temporal rights, could continue to discharge his spiritual powers as Bishop of Rome and head of the universal Church. And, yet again, in less than a day's time, you come here to inform me that the Bishop of Rome and Successor of Peter — a man of eighty years — is to be removed from his city and his See by its so-called liberators. Do not the rights of the Catholic Religion require that he remain here, even if chained within the Vatican, imprisoned like Peter himself? And what of simple justice to an old man? Leave him to die in Rome.

Haller: If he is old and to die, he may do so anywhere. He has no more need to die in Rome than does any man. He is a fallen monarch, condemned by his own people. Exile is a gift! Is it not superior to the guillotine?

Azara: Your fervor is beyond that of any "religious fanatic." I cannot reason with such poison, this so-called "ideology" exported from your Republic. Your appeals to Liberty and Equality are empty without Charity. But I have no power in these matters.

I shall merely convey your intentions and actions to my government.

Cervoni: Ambassador, we shall give His Holiness time to prepare. We shall inform him tomorrow that he is to leave on February 20th. He may take a prelate or cardinal or two with him. He will be sent to the north of Italy. We will allow him, to the extent possible, to choose the place of his exile, where he may live out his days in solitude and peace.

Riganti: Generals, if I may, on behalf of the people of Rome, we, the consuls, ask that you arrange for the pope not only to leave this city, but to leave Italy entirely. Our reasons for the request are the same as those you have given for his removal from Rome. We Romans wish to start anew from this day. But just as the presence of the pope in Rome may impede our progress, his presence in some other part of Italy, perhaps in some part of his former realm, would serve to incite the fanatics who wish to preserve the dead past. Like you, we wish for peace and freedom throughout Italy. To secure it, the pope must leave this peninsula.

Cervoni: Where would you have him go, Consul?

Riganti: We consuls have considered the question, and we believe he should go to Spain. We are confident that his great friend, Ambassador Azara, could arrange for it, and he would be welcomed by the Spanish Crown.

Azara: Are you mad? I have no mandate to remove the pope to Spain! We have no preparations for the journey, let alone for the political and religious upheaval you ask me to provoke. And you want the man out of your country in three days' time? Generals, this is absurd!

Act II, Scene XV

Riganti: Why not Portugal then? We can prepare a ship for the pope and launch it in a few days. Let these Catholic Kingdoms earn their title. The popes once lived at Avignon. Why not now Lisbon?

Berthier: Enough! My orders are plain: the pope is to be removed from Rome and sent to the north of Italy. To the extent possible, he may choose his place of exile. Consuls, you are the elected representatives of the Roman people. You will rule them without the presence of, or interference from, the clerical government. The pope is deposed and will be consigned to residence outside of this city.

Ambassador, you may inform your government accordingly. The pope will be told of his fate tomorrow morning, and he will depart three days thereafter. Prepare accordingly. Good day.

SCENE XVI

At the Vatican

17 FEBRUARY 1798

[*Generals Cervoni and Haller return to the Vatican, where the pope is confined as a prisoner, to deliver the order expelling the pope from Rome.*]

Cervoni: Your Holiness, I trust you know why we are here?

Pius: We have received, General, a correspondence today from Ambassador Azara in which he informs Us of an order under which We are to be exiled from Rome. You have, We see, brought General Haller along with you to deliver the news, a great pleasure for him, no doubt.

Haller: Rather, a great honor it is to deliver the order for your removal, Citizen.

Cervoni: You are directed to leave the city on the morning of 20 February.

Pius: We cannot leave Rome, even if We desired to do so.

Haller: We are aware you that are aged and you are sick, Citizen. Still, we will ensure you are able to travel, perhaps to a climate more to your liking. Have no concern for your ability to leave Rome.

Pius: We did not say, General, that We are physically unable to leave Rome, although it is true that We are old, and sick, and tired. Yet it is not physical limitation, but the mandate of Christ that compels Us to remain. We are not permitted by the duty of

Our office to leave Rome, and We shall not do so. We have told you before that We are the steward of this See. It is Our duty to hand on what We have received. We shall do so to Our successor, who shall occupy this seat when We have gone to Our judgment.

Haller: Your successor? I think not, Citizen Holiness. Do not delude yourself. It is the policy of the Directory that you shall be the last in your line, the last pope. You have no more a successor than did Louis XVI. So put your mind at ease. You have no duty to fulfill.

Pius: Terrible as you are, even if you are, indeed, the very Gates of Hell, you shall not prevail. We fear nothing, save for the judgment of Christ, before whom We shall be surely condemned should We acquiesce to your threats to smash the very rock upon which the Lord Himself founded His Church. Our person is of no consequence, and Our duty remains vested in Us until Our last breath. If it means the frustrations of your pretensions, all the better!

Cervoni: Just as before, Your Holiness, we have pleaded with you to avoid violence, and you have taken every act to maintain the peace. Do not provoke the use of force now. Leave in peace for Tuscany. You may continue your work there.

Pius: You may think so, General, but We believe that your fellow soldiers and your government will disagree. We are aware that, on each concession, another is demanded, under threat of violence, yet called Liberty. We are aware that the goal of the French Republic, by whomever it may be ruled at the moment, is the destruction of the Holy Catholic Religion. For Church will not concede to its ideologies and its demand to place all things under its despotism, though you will call it by other, sweet-sounding names. No, it is Christ who draws all things to Himself, and the Church may not admit otherwise, lest it no longer be the Church. We shall not leave Rome.

Haller: It is the order of the Roman Republic that you leave this city on 20 February 1798. As forces of the allied French Republic, we are bound to carry out the decree of the legitimate government of Rome. You will leave — either voluntarily or by force — but you will leave. How you wish to go is your decision, Citizen Brachi. But your time, and the time of the papacy, is finished. Arrangements will be made for you, so prepare if you wish. We shall return on the morning of the 20th to conduct you from your See.

SCENE XVII

In the Sistine Chapel

THE MORNING OF 19 FEBRUARY 1798

[*With the power of the occupying French army bearing down upon him to force his departure, the pope convenes the Cardinals of the Roman Curia in the Sistine Chapel to discuss the dilemma before him: whether to leave Rome as commanded on the following morning.*]

Pius: Venerable Brethren, We have summoned you here in the sight of the *Last Judgment* to counsel Us on what may well be Our last judgment as Supreme Pontiff. The office of the pope is a strange one: a pope is the Supreme Head of the Church, Her sovereign and Her Legislature. Yet for all his titles and his power, the pope is not as Caesar when he was declared Dictator, or a king as Henry VIII, who may issue pronouncements according to his taste, convenience or will.

The pope is the greatest of sovereigns, in that he holds the very Keys to the Kingdom from Christ Himself, and is at once the lowest of servants, in that he has no powers of his own right, but only those given by Christ for the exercise of the Petrine ministry. The power of the pope is the power to teach as the Apostles taught. The power of the pope is to sanctify all peoples through the governance of the Church, in cooperation with his brother bishops, through the preaching of the Gospel and the distribution of the sacraments. The power of the pope is to confirm, encourage, promote and defend the patrimony of the Church, handed down from the Apostles, through the Fathers, to the great saints of the ages and as set forth by its legitimate general councils of bishops, acting in union with the Holy See.

A pope who would invent a new doctrine would have as much power to do so as a chambermaid. A pope who would express contempt for the Tradition of the Church, in all its varied expressions, would be fit to sit with the Jacobins in Paris. It is a sure sign of the Providence of God that in 18 centuries, no pope, however stupid or sinful, has thought to replace the Creed with his own formula or thought to invent a new Mass according to his own predilections. Who could wear the Ring of the Fisherman and dare to replace the Canon!

Yet, the waves of man's hubris have battered Peter's Barque, ever working to scuttle the ship upon the shoals. Luther's animating cause was the destruction of Peter's successors, preaching that a new Church would arise with the pope cast out. But how can there be a "new Church"? Such a concept is illogical and absurd. A new church would not be *the* Church, with its distinctive marks and its unbroken link to Christ Himself, born on Pentecost Day. Has there been another Pentecost, new and different and better than the first?

Henry Tudor was the harbinger of the irreligious and arbitrary State that wishes to use the Church, or discard the Church, depending on the whim of the secular arm. In our own time, under the guise of the so-called "Enlightenment," even the Catholic powers of Europe have seen fit to degrade the primacy of this Holy See, asserting that the secular power may govern the Church and may fix Her rites and how She may administer them. Seduced by the worship of man's reason alone, forgetting their duties to the Supernatural, they have sought to control, and then destroy, religious life under a claim that they may subordinate even the contemplative worship of Almighty God to their own ends — namely the extension of their arbitrary and unfounded power over the Church, though She is an independent society of divine right to which no sovereign may dictate.

Indeed, the Church precedes the State. She is not the State, nor does She supplant the State, but the authority and existence of the State, to be right and just, flow from the authority of Christ, as transmitted through the Church. To divorce the State from the Church is to offer the State unlimited power, founded on nothing other than the caprice of man. And the great ones shall make their power felt and lord it over them.

But not since Nero has the world seen a lunatic power such as the Jacobins of France. In but 10 years since the King's calling of the Estates General, opened by a Solemn Mass and Procession of the Blessed Sacrament, the Eldest Daughter of Our Mother the Church has fallen into a detestation of Religion resulting in the senseless deaths of thousands, even the deaths of men who championed the glory of the Revolution. They killed their King for his piety and meekness; beheaded their queen and tormented her children; they have massacred priests; they have cut off the heads of nuns. These men have been miserably seduced by an empty phantom of liberty and enslaved by a band of philosophers who contradict and abuse each other.[*]

In an act of counterfeit piety, they, too, have tried to create a "new church", their so-called "Constitutional Church", to be as an arm of the state, an arm severed from the Body of Christ, whose head is the See of Peter, the Guarantor of the Universal Unity of the Faith. And when We refused to permit the priests and bishops to swear an impious "oath" of fidelity to this new church, they said that We would be the cause of a great schism, destroying the unity of the Church. Christ says the Church is to be One, but unity around false principles is tyranny. There is no "Constitutional Church". The Church has a divine constitution, not one conjured *ex nihlio* on a tennis court, but one given by Christ Himself and made effective through Her Tradition.

Now the men who control this once great nation no longer pretend love for the Christian Religion. They admit of their desire to eliminate it. Yet, when Religion dies, what shall replace it? Without Religion, what shall be the bond of society? What, indeed, shall be the purpose to any man's life? The Revolution knows it must answer, and so it would suppress the Christian

---

[*] This sentence is an actual quote attributed to Pius by E.E.Y. Hales in *Revolution and Papacy*, a line the pope uttered to the Curia in his condemnation of the Civil Constitution of the Clergy in 1790.

Faith and in its stead leave the worship of the Revolution itself and its so-called "ideals."

Can man worship an "ideal" or a "notion"? Can he worship what seems a righteous act, or only the One who makes the act righteous? The Revolution claims to bow before "Liberty, Equality and Fraternity." Yet are these not mere words when detached from any source of meaning?

They worship "Liberty" and dance about a tree they call a "Liberty Tree." How sad is this spectacle when contrasted to veneration of the true Liberty Tree, the Wood of the Cross! We venerate the Holy Cross not as an inert, meaningless object, but as the instrument of our very salvation, the means by which God emptied Himself into nothingness. It is the ultimate meaning of man's existence. The Blessed Apostle Paul, writing to our ancestors in this city, preached the liberty wrought by the Cross as the deliverance from sin and corruption that is the essence of the spiritual life. But Christian liberty comes by "groaning", denial and endurance, the subjugation of man to God in obedience.

The Liberty of the Revolution is disobedience, a license to madness, the freedom to destroy those who will not conform to the newly-created morals, and conform again and again when these morals are, again and again, created anew.

They worship Equality, yet men are no more equal under their Revolution than they were under the King. Is General Bonaparte the equal of General Berthier? Is Berthier the equal of Cervoni? Is the guard with his musket at the gates of the Vatican the equal of any or all these men?

Without God, there can be no equality among men. We are not made equal by destroying the station in life to which each man is born or into which he is called by ability, but we are made equal because we are made. We are creatures of God, to whom each and every man owes his duty. The moral law is binding upon all in the same fashion, and all shall face Christ the Just Judge. There is neither Jew nor Greek. We do not worship Equality, yet it is a truth recognizable only in a Christian society.

They worship Fraternity. What is the bond that underlies their brotherhood but some form of fanatical devotion? This, too, is false, an illusion of the mind. "Those who hear the word of God and keep it are my mother and my brothers and my sisters." Their fraternity is but a poor substitute for the greatest of the Theological Virtues. Charity is the abiding quality of the Christian. He does not worship Charity, but rather seeks to imbue all his actions in life according to its rule, as Charity is the rule of Christ.

God is Love. It is in Charity that he seeks to keep the moral law as set down in the Decalogue and as perfected in the Sermon on the Mount, the greatest speech ever delivered. Charity is not honored by abstraction, by the mouthing of a slogan, but by keeping it in daily acts before God and man. Charity is the bond of Perfection, and there can be no justice or right order to society without it. It is the hallmark of Christian society, and the Revolution mocks it with its lofty but empty rhetoric.

Enlightened man, ever searching for the new, the better and the novel, is restless to replace the moral order of God with something that gives a moral order without God. Such folly, the building of a house on sand! They wish to appropriate what is from God and claim that it is instead from man. Ever was it so, since the First Man thought that he should be God. All sin and error have flowed from the same hubris, the same desire to make man into God.

And the man who believes himself God will not hesitate to drop the blade upon the neck of any who will not obey his divinity. Such a man will go ever on wandering, looking for new purpose, some new ideal or cause in which he will find his meaning, tearing down that which he perceives as standing in his way.

But our hearts are restless until they rest in God, says the Doctor of Grace! Man's purpose is in his duty, and his duty is distilled into the Great Commandments: to love, adore and worship God with his whole heart and to love his neighbor as himself. The first of these is the greatest, and from it proceeds the second; they are in essence linked, they cannot be performed, one without the other, and no words or ideas or political causes can ever supplant them as the foundation for man's existence and the source of his meaning.

Against such great error and sin and frenzy stands the Church, whose head We are, both Her sovereign and servant. It is Our charge to preserve this Sacred Ministry, the Petrine Office, regardless of any cost, against any force, trusting in the promise of Our Lord that Hell itself will never prevail over the Church.

To this end, We have solemnly declared before the occupiers and usurpers that We will not leave Rome, despite their commands to the contrary. Each step outside of these walls would bring to Our mind, again and again, two words: *Quo vadis?*

Yet it is true, dear brothers, that We have prayed We would awake from a dream and find that We are alone, at peace and secure from all harm, just as Peter when he came to himself, the chains having dropped from his wrists, outside the gates of the Mamertine Prison. Thus it is fitting that We bring so great a question before you, the Cardinals of the Roman Curia, for your consideration before We make a final decision, for the fate of Rome and the Church Herself may rest upon what We elect to do come dawn tomorrow. Shall the pope leave Rome?

Doria: Your Holiness, I rise to speak as Cardinal Secretary of State and Your Holiness' First Minister. We, your loyal Curia, are humbled before your great courage and unceasing devotion to your scared duties as Successor of Peter. At this terrible hour, nothing remains for us to do but to place our trust, our lives and the life of the Church Herself, into the Providence of Almighty God, who in Christ promised to be with us even unto the end of time.

Whether this is the end, we do not know. And we assembled here agree that our highest purpose is to preserve the Church and secure the succession of Peter until we see the Son of Man coming on the clouds.

There is a great army within our own walls, arrayed against us, and we have no earthly power to repulse it. It seethes with the passion of its masters, whose only desire is to destroy the Church if they are able to devise a way to do so. While it is true that our acquiescence to this point has resulted in greater and more loathsome audacity, it is still the case that Your Holiness lives and that we here assembled have the means at our disposal to secure Your Holiness' life and thereby to secure time in order to work for the continuation of the Petrine ministry, whether it is seated in Rome, or Antioch, or some other See where his chair may be set.

Thus, it is my judgment that Your Holiness commits no dereliction in leaving this city. Leaving on the morrow is the last hope to avoid violence against your people, and perhaps even your own death. We, your brothers, know that Your Holiness does not flee merely to save your own life or out of any fear of physical suffering. We also know that, in the name of the Church, we must ensure that Your Holiness lives. Your death now, and the undoubted suppression of all Religion that would surely follow, could prevent the Sacred College from convening at all, and the line of popes would be smashed.

Thus, not for fear, not for weakness, but for the good of the Church, I humbly submit to this body that His Holiness should leave Rome for Tuscany tomorrow morning, as the French command. We must pray that His Holiness may continue to carry out his ministry from there and that we who are left here are able to carry on the work of the Roman Curia in his absence.

Your Eminence, Cardinal Somaglia, Vicar of Rome, what say you?

Cardinal Somaglia: I say that what is of the Revolution is the work of the devil! I say that the French wish to do to the Vatican what Titus did to the Temple, and then to erect a new pagan cult above the bones of St. Peter! May God cast down from their thrones such impious men!

And I say, as Cardinal Vicar of Rome, that Your Holiness must leave the city. Only God can stop the French now, and I cannot bear that thought of Your Holiness' further suffering at the hands of the wicked. I, too, believe that we must try to carry on with prudence. Resistance would only grant another excuse — another death of Duphot — for the French to destroy us.

Go, Your Holiness, and trust in the Lord our Protector.

Pius: Is this, then, the will of the Curia, that We go as commanded tomorrow?

[*all the Cardinals stand*]

Doria: Yes, Your Holiness, we beg you to take this course.

Pius: A pope must rule only with the advice of his Cardinals, lest he allow his own mind to think contrary to the mind of the Church. Abandoned to the inscrutable will of Lord, and as the Servant of the Servants of God, We submit to your wise counsel. We shall leave Rome tomorrow. We shall weep for Rome, as the Lord wept for Jerusalem, and pray God that We shall see it again.

SCENE XVIII

At the Vatican

BEFORE DAWN, 20 FEBRUARY 1798[*]

[*At four o'clock on the morning of Monday, February 20, 1798, the pope heard Mass inside St. Peter's for the last time, while a carriage waited outside of the Apostolic Palace to take him from Rome. Cardinal Doria Pamphili offers the Mass, and, at its close, turns to the frail pope, standing to the side of the altar* in choro.]

Doria: [*standing at the Gospel side of the Altar, completing the Proclamation of the Last Gospel of the Mass*]: Et Verbum Caro Factum Est, et habitavit in nobis, et vidimus gloriam eius, gloriam quasi Unigeniti a Patre, plenum gratiae et veritatis.

Pius: Deo gratias.[†]

[*Doria returns to the center of the altar and, at the tabernacle, removes a small piece of the Sacred Host, enclosing it in a small, round pyx to which is attached a simple string so that the pyx may be worn around the neck. He takes the pyx to the pope.*]

Doria: Your Holiness, I know they have taken every possession from you, even your breviary, but what could be of more use and value to you on the journey than the tiny particle enclosed inside this pyx?

Pius: This is the living bread come down from Heaven. There is no need for any other provision. [*the pope places the Pyx around*

---

[*] Pastor recounts the pope's refusal to turn over the Ring of the Fisherman, and his leaving a dawn with the Sacred Host around his neck.
[†] The final lines of the "Last Gospel", the closing rite of the Mass, taken from St. John, "And the Word became flesh and dwelt among us, and we saw his glory, the glory of the Only-Begotten Son of the Father, full of grace and truth."

his neck and conceals it within his cassock] Thank you, Doria, for this kindness and blessing.

Doria: There is a carriage here, Your Holiness, in the Cortile di San Damaso. Monsignor Caracciolo, Your Holiness' chief chamberlain and most loyal servant, unhesitatingly agreed to accompany you in the carriage, as has your secretary Fr. Marotti. Perhaps the only good that has come from the suppression of the Jesuits is Marotti's transfer from the Company of Ignatius to the service of Your Holiness.*

Pius: Loyola thought of his Company as the soldiers of the pope. It seems that We have lived to witness the consequence of a sovereign disbanding his own army. We shall take solace in the company of these clerics, who sacrifice everything to give comfort to Our ailing body and sorrowful soul.

Doria, We charge you now, in Our last act within these walls, to take care to see that the Sacred College continues to carry out the governance of the Church, just as before, and that most especially, the Cardinals make every preparation possible for the next conclave. There must be a successor, immediately, on Our death, and Our time is now short.

Doria: You have made wise provision, Your Holiness, for these affairs. The Special Congregation of six cardinals that you established will ably govern in your absence, even if you should be forced to abdicate.†

Pius: Resign the Petrine Office? That, Your Eminence, is beyond Our countenance. We have ceded all that We possibly can, even Rome itself, but never shall We voluntarily resign the

---

* Marotti was a former Jesuit, a priest of the Society of Jesus, the order disastrously suppressed at the behest of the Catholic sovereigns of Europe by Pius' predecessor, Clement XIV.

† Pastor notes, again, Pius' concern that the cardinals elect a successor and his erection of a governing council of six to rule in his absence.

Act II, Scene XVIII　　　　　　　　　　　　　　　　　　　　　　105

mandate given by Christ through the Church. Our death is Our resignation. Instruct the Cardinals accordingly.
Now, Doria, it is time.

[*The pope and Doria make their way to the square outside the Apostolic Palace where the pope's carriage awaits. At the carriage stand Msgr. Caracciolo, Fr. Marotti, Dr. Tassi, the pope's personal physician, and a few servants. French troops are present to escort the carriage out of the city, along with Generals Cervoni and Haller.*]

Haller: Good morning, Citizens! And a fine morning it is for your last in Rome. Sadly, it is still too dark for the citizens of the city to cheer as they see your carriage pass through the gates!

Pius: Everything done in the darkness shall be brought into the light. And when that fearful day comes for you General, We shall pity you indeed.

Haller: He maintains his pretensions to the end. And what's this I see? This man still wears rings upon his fingers? I thought we had stripped him of his ill-gotten wealth. Hand those rings to my men this instant!

Pius: General, do you think We care for such things? You are a greater fool than We supposed. One you may have. Do with it as you wish, for it is Our own possession and Ours to give. The other you shall have to cut from Our finger if you wish to touch it at all, as it is not Ours, but Peter's own ring, and it goes to Our successor.

Haller: Then hand it to me, by all means, for this army, this republic is your successor, Citizen.

Cervoni: It is time, Your Holiness. Leave the Fishman's Ring upon your hand. How it shall come into the possession of another pope I cannot say, but you may take with your faith.

Pius: Like the Devil Himself, General, it seems you would put the Lord Your God to the test. But His ways are not your ways. We trust in the guarantee of Christ; you, in the whims of the Directory.

Haller: It is our whim that you leave. Your carriage, Citizen, is ready. Farewell!

Pius [*raising his right hand*]: Let all here present know that We forgive these men for their grievous acts against Us. May they repent before God. And We impart upon all here, and upon this city, eternal possession of the Successors of Peter, Our Apostolic Blessing. *Benedicat Vos Omnipotens Deus, Pater, et Filius, et Spiritus Sanctus. Amen.* [*the carriage departs*]

Act III
THE POPE IN EXILE

The Death of His Holiness Pius VI in the Citadel of Valence, 28 August 1799, engraving by A. Campanella after J. Beys, 1802.

SCENE I

At the Certosa, the Carthusian Monastery, Florence
15 FEBRUARY, 1799*

[*On his departure from Rome, the pope was first sent to Siena in the Grand Duchy of Tuscany. The pope, in poor health and nearly unable to walk or stand, was held at Siena until the end of May, 1798. At that time, the puppet-government at Rome agreed to permit the pope to reside, temporarily, in the Carthusian monastery, known as the Certosa (Charterhouse), just outside of Florence, capital of the Grand Duchy.*]

[*A year into his exile, the pope is confined to the Certosa, along with his few companions, including Monsignor Spina, who has replaced the pope's nephew as his principal aid.*]

Spina: Good morning, Holy Father. I bring you news today.

Pius (from his bed): I suppose, Spina, you are going to tell me they have at last commanded that I be taken to a ship and left upon the shores of Sardinia to die. Is this to be, at last, my ship from Delos, bearing the hemlock, like the one that was the harbinger of Socrates' demise?

Spina: No, Your Holiness, even the French recognize your feeble state. There is no question now of a sea voyage to Sardinia in your present condition. Here, in the Certosa, we remain.

Pius: What is then, Spina? I am perhaps to be allowed to resume a daily walk, if I ever recover my legs?

---

* Based upon Pastor's account of the events that occurred on the pope's anniversary and shortly thereafter; also based upon his account of the content of the Bull of 13 November 1798. The pope and his companions were constantly threatened with exile to the island of Sardinia, and the French had even denied Pius the right to a daily walk.

Spina: I am afraid I have received no such permission for you, Holy Father. But it seems that you have forgotten the day.

Pius: I have forgotten many days, Monsignor. I am confined here with so few visitors, so little news, so little ability to discharge my duty and my right to govern the Church. But, forgive me Spina, for I do not wish to waste our precious time together on such complaints. Help me, now to the chair.

Spina: Today, Your Holiness, this humble chair shall be the Cathedra of the Roman Pontiff! [*helping the pope to his chair and turning towards the door*] Bring in the altar! [*two men enter carrying a small portable altar and set it down before the pope in his chair*]

Pius: An altar, here?! *Mirabile Dictu!*

Spina: Today is the 24th anniversary of Your Holiness' coronation as Sovereign Pontiff. And this occasion shall be marked, as it must be marked, by the celebration of Holy Mass with the attendant ceremonies giving thanks to God for your reign.

Pius: It has been a year, then, Spina, since we sang out the *Te Deum* for the last time in St. Peter's. We praised and thanked God for the gift of the Petrine Ministry at the very hour that the Jacobins declared the end of the papacy. It is among His mysteries that We have reigned for so long! Here, infirm, immobile, a prisoner in a monastery far from Rome, God permits Our stewardship of His Church to continue. His ways are truly inscrutable, and yet, in these perils, We have nothing within Our heart but joyous thanksgiving in this shabby cell.

Spina: Michelangelo, son of Florence though he was, never touched this room, but today it is as blessed as the Basilica of St. Peter itself because you, the Holy Father, are here, and Christ is here with us in the Unbloody Sacrifice. You have now

Act III, Scene I

governed the Church for longer than any pope since St. Peter himself. Perhaps no other was so indispensable for Her survival.

Pius: What is indispensable is the Petrine Ministry, so essential is it to the nature of the Church. The only care left for Us in this world is Our work to ensure that We shall have a successor, elected properly and freely by the Cardinals, without the tyranny of the secular powers or the Jacobins' interference.

Spina: Your new Bull of 13 November, 1798 on the election of your successor was warmly received by the Cardinals. It will guide them when the time comes, Your Holiness.

Pius: Remember, Spina, that the point of the Bull is the speed and legitimacy of the election. We charge you, Spina! See that the Cardinals follow its instructions. Where they shall meet, and how many shall be able to convene, God alone knows. You must follow the law as laid down by the Bull of 13 November: in whatever territory of a Catholic ruler the greatest number of electors is able to meet, there shall be the legitimate conclave.

Do not concern yourselves with ceremony, or with competition for the location of the conclave. We pray it shall be in Rome! But, if Rome remains under the tyranny of the Jacobins, the conclave must find another home, even outside Italy if circumstances warrant. It must be under the jurisdiction of a Catholic sovereign who will not seek to meddle in it, who will respect the sacredness and absolute secrecy that befits the election of the Roman Pontiff. The valid conclave will be the one attended by the greatest number of the Sacred College. The Cardinal Dean, or whichever cardinal in attendance is senior, shall arrange for the voting and procedures given the circumstances the Cardinals encounter.

They must adhere to the Bull, Spina. They must elect a successor with legal legitimacy, quickly, and proclaim his election and coronation to the whole world. This is Our last command as pontiff, and We shall repeat it until Our final breath.

Spina: I shall do everything in my power to carry out the wishes of Your Holiness. Your Cardinals love you, Holy Father, and share in your misery, and in your hope for the Church. They will obey the Bull. They will elect a successor.

Indeed, their love and concern for Your Holiness is evident in the correspondence I have lately received from Cardinal Antonelli, acting as he does as your chief minister at Rome. He is grieved to learn that Your Holiness has been deprived of the ability to offer Mass, and even to receive the Sacrament. I have informed Cardinal Antonelli of Your Holiness' condition, your inability to stand, and he has responded that, in the opinion of the Cardinals in Rome, Your Holiness should be permitted to offer Mass from your chair. Pope Benedict XIV said Mass seated in his infirmity. Your Holiness should do likewise! The paramount concern is that Your Holiness take the Sacrament frequently, for your spiritual well-being is of the utmost concern to the Church.

Pius: Monsignor, We are indebted to you for your service, and especially for your arranging this celebration to mark the anniversary of Our coronation. We rejoice not for Ourself, but for the Church, for even amidst the darkness shines the Light, a Light that the darkness still does not comprehend.

But, no, Monsignor, as much as We are desirous of the Sacrament, We shall not permit Ourself an indult to offer the Mass from a chair. It is not for the Roman Pontiff to provide excuses for the derogation from the rubrics of the Mass. All priests are bound to the red, as much as to the black, and the pope is no less so obligated. Indeed, it is among Our most solemn duties to safeguard in every aspect the Roman Missal. The pope carries out his most august public function in offering the Holy Mass and must exemplify for the Church the care and subservience due to the priestly function at the altar.

In comparison to such an imperative, Our personal convenience, and personal limitations, are of no matter whatever. It does not belong to the pope to re-fashion the Mass according to his own tastes and circumstances. He is the servant of the Mass, not its master; its custodian, not its creator.

Should it be known in Rome that the even the pope himself offers Mass from a chair, it will only encourage excuses, laziness and abuses against which the Roman Pontiff is the chief guardian. We should rather go without the Sacrament than to offer the Holy Sacrifice in an unworthy manner, lest it be the cause of scandal or excuse for Our brethren.

So We thank the Cardinals for their solicitude, but We do not agree that it is permissible to offer the Mass from a chair, whether it be the throne of St. Peter's or this lowly piece of wood here in this cell.[*]

Spina: Yes, Holy Father, I shall do as you command. And now, with your permission, I shall vest and offer the Mass in your presence.

Pius: *Corpus Domini Nostri Iesu Christi Custodiat Animam Meam in Vitam Aeternam. Amen!* [†]

---

[*] Pastor recounts that Cardinal Antonelli wrote to the pope in March 1799, urging his frequent Communion and suggesting that he offer Mass from a chair. The pope rejected the idea.

[†] The traditional prayer said by the priest before receiving Holy Communion at Mass: "May the Body of Our Lord Jesus Christ preserve my soul to everlasting life."

SCENE II

Inside the Hotel du Gouvernement at Valence, France
28 AUGUST, 1799[*]

[*In April 1799, the relentless Directory forced the pope from his residence at the Certosa outside of Florence into a three-month journey through northern Italy—Bologna, Parma, Piacenza, Turin—and finally across the Alps into France at Briançon. From there, he was pushed on to Grenoble and, finally, to the small city of Valence, where he was imprisoned in the citadel of the city within a building known as the Hôtel du Gouvernement.*]

[*Here, the sickly and nearly-paralyzed pope arrived on 14 July, 1799, 10 years to the day after the fall of the Bastille. Here, six weeks later, he would come, at last, to the end of his journey into exile.*]

Spina [*at the bedside of the pope*]: Holy Father, I regret that these vestments we have given you are so faded and shabby, but the chasuble in which we have clothed you is the only one we could manage to find in the town.

Pius: It matters not, Spina. You have, as always, done as We have asked to the best of your abilities under these poor conditions. It is an immeasurable comfort to Us that, as We approach Our final hour, We are clothed in the armor of Christ, the vestments of the priest. We wish to die a priest. Now, Spina, bring the Sacrament and my Bible, and gather together Msgr. Caracciolo and Fr. Marotti.

---

[*] The account of the pope's death is taken from Pastor's description, wherein he notes the pope's specific request for burial at Rome as well as his profession of Faith.

Spina [*dons a stole and open pyx containing a Consecrated Host*]: I am ready Your Holiness. Msgr. Caracciolo and Fr. Marotti have just entered the room.

Caracciolo: We are here, Holy Father, to watch and pray with you.

Pius: May you not fall asleep, Caracciolo! Not on my account, but on account of the Church. The cup is soon to pass from me, and I shall be judged. But this bitter chalice will be handed to you, who must bear the burden to secure the Faith. It is I who should pray for you. And, now dear brothers, a final request: We ask to be returned to Rome, to be buried in hallowed ground, in the city of St. Peter, as befits the line of his successors. The pope must live, and reign, die and rest at Rome. We ask you, brothers, to discharge this last request, with all of your devotion to Us. Now, the Bible, please, Spina. [*Placing his hand on the Bible*]

In the presence of this company and before Almighty God, We hereby solemnly profess that We hold, believe and profess all of the doctrine and dogmatic teachings of the Holy Roman Catholic Church, as given from Our Lord Jesus Christ Himself to the Holy Apostles, whose successor We are, and We hereby affirm all that is set forth in the Deposit of the Faith, the deposit, by the Grace of God, it is Our duty to protect and hand on, and We entrust Our life entirely to the Incarnation, Birth, Death and Resurrection of Our Lord Jesus Christ, who is both God and man, the Second Person of the Blessed Trinity, who shall come again to judge the world He made.

And now, let us prepare for the Communion.

Confiteor Deo omnipotenti, beatae Maria semper Virgini, beato Michaeli Archangelo, beato Ioanni Baptistae, sanctis Apostolis Petro and Paulo, omnibus Sanctis, et vobis, fratres: qui peccavi nimis cogitatione, verbo et opere: mea culpa, mea culpa, mea maxima culpa. Ideo precor beatam Mariam semper Virginem, beatum Michaelem Archangelum, beatum Ioannem Baptistam, sanctos Aposotlos Petrum et Paulum, omnes Sanctos, et vos, fratres, orare pro me ad Dominium, Deum nostrum.

Act III, Scene II   117

Caracciolo: Misereatur tui omnipotens Deus, et dimissis peccatis tuis, perducat te ad vitam aeternam.

Pius: Amen.

Caracciolo: Indulgentiam, absolutionem et remissionem peccatorum nostrorum trubuat nobis omnipotens et misericors Dominus.

Pius: Amen.*

Spina [*approaches the pope's bed, holding the Sacred Host before the pope*]: Corpus Domini Nostri Iesu Christi cusodiat animam tuam in vitam aeternam. Amen. [*the pope receives the Sacrament*]

> [*With the pope's Communion, all kneel and begin to recite the Prayers for the Dying. The pope is given a crucifix to hold. He closes his eyes.*]

Pius: [*crying out*]: Father, forgive them! [*Raising his hand, holding the crucifix*]. Benedicat vos omnipotens Deus: Pater, et Filius, et Spiritus Sanctus. Amen. [*the crucifix drops from his hand*]†

Caracciolo: Consumatum est. It is finished. He is at last at peace, just as the sun rises this 29th day of August, Feast of the Passion of St. John the Baptist.

Spina: How many heads have been cut off by the Herods of our time who rule as tyrannically as he who commanded John's head on a platter? His Holiness was spared the blade, but is no less a martyr than the Baptist.

---

* The traditional *Confiteor* prayer of the Mass, the public confession and absolution from sin, is prayed by the priest and servers during the prayers at the foot of the altar and then again before the Communion of the Faithful.
† Pastor quotes the pope as having uttered these words, and says he imparted the blessing holding the crucifix, as his last words before death.

Caracciolo: Both died a prisoner for the truth of Christ, at the hands of the state which wishes only to destroy it. We must pledge ourselves to his last wish, Spina. We must see to it that his remains are transferred to Rome. All of his energies in exile were given over to secure the survival of the papacy, and thus the survival of the Church Herself. Even in death, he knew the pope must be at Rome.

Spina: Pius VI is in exile still. But, by the grace of God, he shall cross the Alps one last time.

SCENE III
At Valence, Spina and Napoleon
11 OCTOBER, 1799*

[*Following his death, the pope's remains were locked in a small chapel inside the* Hôtel du Gouvernement. *The Directory would permit not even a burial, let alone transfer of the body to Rome. True to the wishes of their master, Spina and Caracciolo remained at Valence, working to secure custody of the pope's body.*]

[*On 9 October 1799, General Napoleon Bonaparte, on his return from his campaign in Egypt, landed on the southern cost of France at Saint-Raphael. From there, he made his way with haste north towards Paris to confront the Directory and the increasingly chaotic political situation. Two days after landing, Napoleon passed through Valence, where he invited Spina to accompany him on a carriage ride during his short stay in the city.*]

Napoleon: I hope you will enjoy our ride together, Monsignor. I am pleased to be back in France and I trust we will enjoy each other's company. It seems we have both endured long campaigns.

Spina: You have known nothing but war, General, for several years. I have known nothing but flight. I have gone into Egypt, with the Holy Father and the whole Church, and you have returned from there. Perhaps, General, when you reach Paris, you will help lead us out of Egypt too?

---

* Pastor notes Napoleon's arrival in Valence and his meeting with Spina, whom he promises to assist. Spina formed a friendship with the general following their encounter in Valence, and he would go on to play an important role in the great struggle between Pius VII and Napoleon in the coming years.

Napoleon: I have received reports of the events in Rome and the travails of the pope. I have no wish to continue to malign the Church. I am a Catholic, and Catholicism is the Religion of the French people. My uncle, my mother's brother, is a Cardinal of the Roman Church, as you surely know.

Spina: Then, General, you realize the present state of the Church is intolerable. You know that this lunatic campaign to destroy Religion must end.

Napoleon: When I was in Italy, Monsignor, did I not spare Rome, against the orders of the Directory? Did I not leave unmolested the temporal rights of the pope? There was a pope, and there should be a pope again. Such is fitting for the tranquility of France and all Europe.

Spina: Then you will help us, General, to restore the rights of the Christian Religion in France and wherever the Revolution has taken hold in Europe?

Napoleon: Were it for me to decide, the Church would indeed have Her rights restored. Religion is necessary and salutary for good order, and I would have no wish to deprive the people of it. The rights of the Church of which you speak, Monsignor, are spiritual rights and, when exercised under the proper auspices of the state, will give rise to harmony.

Spina: And what of the papacy, General?

Napoleon: As I said, Monsignor, the pope may reign, and should reign — on matters spiritual. Has there not always been a pope and an emperor, the ecclesial and the civil power? Charlemagne, a Frank, made it so, and I see our present French Empire as the heir to his legacy — uniting Europe under one system, into which the Church will be incorporated.

Act III, Scene III 121

Spina: But it was the pope who crowned Charlemagne. The Church gave sanction to the state. In your system, are they to be equals, the ecclesial power and the civil?

Napoleon: I suggest they are separate powers. Both necessary, but each must act within its own jurisdiction. The Church cannot overmaster the state. Rather, the Church, as the promoter of the virtuous citizen, is at the service of the state. With this understanding, I would see the Church prosper in France, indeed, in the whole of Europe. She is the mistress of the spiritual realm, while the state looks to the general good order of society.

Spina: Then, General, for the good of the whole society, you admit that there should be, must be, a successor of Peter at Rome.

Napoleon: A pope who can accept the proper role of the Church would be most welcome in a new Europe, free from the constant turbulence. There have been excesses, Monsignor, in the zeal to build such a new world, and I would restore Religion to its rightful place. We shall see if Providence truly favors the Church, for I understand that there is yet no conclave in session.

Spina: Your government has seen fit to make it as difficult as possible to elect a successor to Pope Pius. Can you break the seals affixed to the doors of the Sistine, General, so that the Sacred College might undertake its divine duty?

Napoleon: Ha! I have business at Paris, indeed, Monsignor, but I have no intention to raise such a request at the moment. Setting affairs right with the Directory is the immediate task. Yet, do not underestimate me, sir. I shall see to the matters of the Church in due time. Until then, you will have to rely on God's favor, not the power of one man, to choose a new pope.

Spina: Still, there is a matter of urgency you might raise with the Directory. I have remained here at Valence with some brethren for one purpose — to secure the return of the body of the pope to Rome. Since the Holy Father died over a month ago, we have been forbidden even to enter the chamber of the chapel where they have locked his mortal remains. It is a manifest injustice, General, that the body of the Vicar of Christ is deprived of a consecrated resting place.

Worse still, it was His Holiness' last wish that his body be returned to Rome and buried with the Successors of Peter. How can you speak of the restoration of Religion while the body of the Vicar of Christ on Earth lies in a darkened room without the most humble memorial to his rank and his service?

Napoleon: What brought the pope to so sad an end, Monsignor? It was not his fault that the world around him was changed so greatly, that the new ideas took hold. He was a man of the world, of learning and good birth. Surely he knew that the Church, to survive, would have to give way to the secular powers, to republicanism and egalitarian ideas. He could have saved his spiritual throne had he acquiesced before the civil power, recognized it and legitimized it.

Instead, in his obstinacy, as an old man, he chose suffering and exile, and nonetheless witnessed the subjugation of the Church and the loss of his temporal power. He was, in the end, an impractical man.

Spina: You believe that, for the sake of the practical, the Church may cede this power, this point, this right, this tradition, and yet remain, in essence, the Church. Would such a practical course truly preserve the Church, as you suggest? I am afraid, General, the pope was wiser than you presume with your practicality.

Napoleon: I wonder if any wise prince ends his days as a prisoner in exile. I am not without pity, Monsignor. I shall see about your master's return to Rome, despite his folly.

Spina: Is it folly to give all one has for the Faith? Can your government be so miserly as to deny the meager request of a few humble clerics, bereft of our master, that we might take his body to a place of final rest?

Ah, I see we are approaching the Hotel. Thank you for this drive, General. Perhaps we will talk on these matters again.

Napoleon: I assure you we will, Monsignor. And, should there be another pope, be sure to send him my greetings. I have no doubt that, should there be another Pius, he will wish to consider a better way for the Church in the future.

Spina: And you shall have a way to propose to him, I trust?

Napoleon: That, as you might say, is in God's hands. I shall be watching across the Alps for the white smoke.

Spina: Keep your eyes fixed, General. And if there is a new Pius, you will do well to remember the old one. For he knew something of more value, of more strength than you conceive: *Again, the kingdom of Heaven is like unto a merchant seeking good pearls, who when he found one pearl of great price, went his way, sold all he had, and bought it.*

EPILOGUE

The exile of Pius VI from Rome did not end until 17 February 1802 when, four years after he stepped into the carriage that took him from the Eternal City, his mortal remains were carried into St. Peter's in solemn procession. Monsignor Spina, true to his duty, saw to the removal of Pius' body from Valence on Christmas Eve, 1801, and accompanied it across the Alps once more, returning the late pope home by the same route over which he had been driven into banishment, down through Tuscany, passing by Florence and Siena, the places where he had suffered under house arrest. On 18 February 1802, Pius, at last, received the Solemn Requiem he desired in the papal basilica.

Pius VI, perhaps, would have thought his papacy a success simply because, after all that had transpired, his requiem was offered in the presence of his successor, who stood at the throne and who pronounced the traditional absolution over the catafalque at the close of the Solemn Mass. Pius VI was not the last pope.

The conclave that elected the successor to the "last pope" opened on the feast of the first Apostle, St. Andrew, the man who brought Peter to Christ, 30 November, 1799. As Pius feared, the cardinals could not convene at Rome, but, under the protection of the Austrians, the Sacred College managed to assemble on the tiny island of San Giorgio, off of Venice, where the Order of St. Benedict welcomed 34 cardinals into its monastery of St. Gregory the Great. After months of deadlock, on 14 March 1800, the cardinals elected as pope a member of the same order under whose hospitality they labored, the Benedictine cardinal-bishop of Imola, Gregory Barnabas Chiaramonte.

Ironically, it was Cardinal Chiaramonte who three years earlier had worked to reconcile the so-called Revolutionary ideals and the Christian life in his Christmas sermon of 1797.

Now, despite his conciliatory disposition, the cardinal took the name Pius in honor of his defiant predecessor.

Pope Pius VII was destined to endure even greater, longer and more complex trials than had Pius VI. Through these physical and spiritual challenges, he remained a man instinctively committed to the vision of his Christmas sermon, a pope who wished to find a way for the Church to live at peace with the New Order, and yet remain the Church. His amazing 14-year-long contest with Napoleon lasted from the moment of his election as pontiff until the last minutes before Napoleon's abdication. Despite his longing for harmony, Pius VII, who accepted the invitation to crown Napoleon emperor at Paris, would later excommunicate Bonaparte and suffer years of isolated imprisonment at his hands in a struggle to preserve the independence and spiritual integrity of the Church.

The state of the Church in our own time, and how it became so, is unintelligible without knowledge of the history of the Prisoner Popes, Pius VI and Pius VII. May their stories be told, and may their successors honor their legacy.

BIBLIOGRAPHY

Abbot, John S.C. *The Story of Joseph Bonaparte*, New York: Harper & Brothers Publishers, 1902.

Azara, Jose Nicolas. *Epistolario of Jose Nicolas de Azara (1784-1804)*. Buenos Aires: Nueva Bibliotec de Erudicion y Critica, 2013.

Azara, Jose Nicolas. *Memorias*. Madrid: Bibliotecario-Anticuario de la Biblioteca Nacional de Madrid, 1847.

Bonaparte, Napoleon. *Correspondance de Napoléon Ier. Tome 3*. Paris: Originally published by order of Emperor Napoleon III, 1858-1869; online version published by Bibliothèque nationale de France, département Philosophie, histoire, sciences de l'homme, 2012.

Duppa, Richard. *A Journal of the Most Remarkable Occurrences that Took Place in Rome, Upon the Subversion of the Ecclesiastical Government, in 1798*. London: G.G. and J. Robinson, 1799.

Hales, E.E.Y. *Revolution and Papacy*. London: Eyre & Spottiswoode, 1960.

Pastor, Ludwig. *The History of the Popes from the Close of the Middle Ages: Pius VI 1775-1799*.

Perigord, Charles Maurice de Talleyrand. *La Confession de Talleyrand V. 1-5 Memoires du Prince de Talleyrand* (Public Domain).

Wornonoff, Denis. *The Thermindorean Regime and the Directory 1794-1799*. Cambridge: Cambridge University Press, 1984.

ABOUT THE AUTHOR

Christian Browne is a graduate of Regis High School in New York City, the College of the Holy Cross (Worcester, MA), and Fordham University School of Law. He is a partner in a law firm based in Long Island, New York where he practices in the areas of civil litigation, land use law and real estate transactions. He has contributed articles on Church history and liturgical matters to *Crisis Magazine* and the website Onepeterfive.com.

Mr. Browne lives in Rockville Centre, New York with his wife Lauren Ann and their four children, Joseph Ignatius, Agnes Elizabeth, Peter Aquinas and Felicity Ann Browne.